Historiography

Historiography

Past and Present

EDITORS
Kirit K. Shah
Meherjyoti Sangle

RAWAT PUBLICATIONS
Jaipur • New Delhi • Bangalore • Guwahati • Kolkata

ISBN 978-81-7033-956-4

First Published, 2005

Reprinted, 2017

Published by
Prem Rawat for **Rawat Publications**
Satyam Apts., Sector 3, Jawahar Nagar, Jaipur 302 004 (India)
Phone: 0141 265 1748 / 7006 Fax: 0141 265 1748
E-mail: info@rawatbooks.com
Website: www.rawatbooks.com

New Delhi Office
4858/24, Ansari Road, Daryaganj, New Delhi 110 002
Phone: 011 - 23263290

Also at *Bangalore, Guwahati* and *Kolkata*

Typeset by Rawat Computers, Jaipur
Printed at Nice Printing Press, New Delhi

Contents

Acknowledgements

Diverse are the origins of the papers put together here and so we will have to acknowledge our debt to each contributor as per the context in which he/she responded to our request on the theme assigned. In origin, the paper of Pushpa Bhave is the script of the First Shanta Gambhir Memorial Lecture, which she delivered in the University Department of History, SNDT Women's University, Mumbai on September 27, 2002. We thank her here for having accepted our invitation, and drafting the lengthy script of her scholarly lecture.

In organizing the seminar on "Historiography: Changing Paradigms and Parameters" our fundamental problem was that of funds. Ours was not even what is usually called a shoestring budget. Our former senior colleague from sociology came forward and offered a generous donation. We place on record our gratitude to Jyoti Vora for this noble contribution.

The keynote to any seminar always represents its broad thematic focus and Aniket Jaaware's contribution more than fulfilled our expectations.

The Seminar being bilingual, the publication of the proceedings posed peculiar problems. Only Raja Dixit accepted the task of translating his paper from Marathi to English and that, too, within the very short time limit we gave him, setting aside his other commitments. We feel indebted to him. In other cases, contributors were unwilling to translate or revise their script within the date fixed. Naturally, we had to request other scholars to do the necessary, and they responded very kindly and honoured our deadline. We place on record our deep sense of gratitude to Radhika Seshan, Chhaya Goswami, C.R. Das, and Umesh Kadam, and also to Jatin Wagle and Dr Aravind Ganachari, who were our resource persons for the Seminar.

We deeply regret the delay in publishing the papers, which partly resulted from the fact that the script of two presentations needed to be transcribed from their taped versions, a process not easy to handle. Further, the script so prepared needed to be approved by the concerned speakers. We are truly touched by the kind consent of Maithreyi Krishnaraj to not only go through our version of her presentation, but also substantially redesign and rewrite it.

To our colleague Jaswandi Wamburkar, we are grateful for all the labour she put in to organize the First Shanta Gambhir Memorial Lecture and render us all the required cooperation in organizing the Seminar.

Our students and the Post-Graduate Studies and Research Department office-staff are always the backbone of any programme that we plan. We can hardly name them all. Our gratitude to them is nonetheless heartfelt. So also to our respective families, for all the support we have received through the long period from planning the Seminar to publishing its proceedings.

The final editing of the script involved a lot of work in terms of keeping the patterns of referencing uniform and locating and removing errors and ambiguities. Our young colleague, Neelambari Jagtap, offered to undertake the taxing task of preparing the copy for the press, soft as well as hard, and thereby helped avoid further delay in bringing out this already delayed book. We appreciate her willing cooperation.

March 24, 2005

Kirit K. Shah
Meherjyoti Sangle

Introduction

Kirit K. Shah and Meherjyoti Sangle

The opening sentence of the introduction to the UGC Model Curriculum on *History and Archaeology* reads, "The past remains constant, but writings about the past change".[1] This eternal and irreconcilable dichotomy between the past in the absolute and its relative character in the representations that are done down the ages constitutes the theme uniting the anthology of articles edited here. Ever since its introduction as an independent discipline, history teaching in higher education in India has been dominated by the dynastic model, which treats non-political dimensions as secondary or supplementary to the main narrative and are broken up in accordance with breaks in the chronology of the political narrative. In fact, even the books by eminent historians prescribed for study by the students were conceived and written on this pattern, contributing to a perception of the past in which changes in socioeconomic and cultural domains of life run parallel to the political. In addition to this fundamental flaw, the prescribed curriculum hardly ever offered courses of study on the philosophy and methodology of history even at the postgraduate stage. As a result, the student rarely realized the relative character of past reality in the representations she was made to study, getting confused by the multiple and often contradictory interpretations of the same historical fact. Again, the powerful projection of the past in the electronic media and intense attacks mounted by the postmodernists on the claims of authenticity and objectivity affirmed by historians for their accounts have virtually created an existential crisis, compelling the community of historians to do some self-introspection so as to evolve the required responses to the challenges confronting them and to impart an open-ended character to the practice of the discipline.

Possibly against this background, the UGC Committee on Model Curriculum in History and Archaeology designed papers on Historiography in such a manner as to depart from the earlier practice of confining them only to the biography and contribution of prominent historians. A clear emphasis now is to initiate the student into models and methods of history, old as well as new, so as to equip her to understand the phenomenon of multiple perspectives on the past in place of the 'grand narrative', as of yore. However, effecting radical change in the curriculum has to go hand in hand with offering solutions to the problems of changeover, the most fundamental of these being the availability of ready, high quality course material and orientation of teachers alien to the multidisciplinary territory they are supposed to cover for effective teaching. This is precisely the context in which the present collection originated as some of the papers were presented at a seminar organized by the SNDT Women's University, Department of History, Mumbai for the orientation of teachers and students. The papers are, by their very purpose and content, freelance essays rather than research papers on the themes assigned to the resource persons with a request to give only a broad understanding of salient concepts, processes, and features of the models for an *average student*, appending at the end a basic bibliography for further reading and referencing. Since an average student of history is ill-equipped to learn lessons in meta-history, the scholars were specifically asked to simplify the subtle and serious aspects of their themes, concretizing in the process as much of the abstract as possible.

While it was imperative to have an article on each model, it was equally important to have one covering all or most of them, in the nature of the journey of history along its own track with milestones in terms of the new paradigms and parameters from old to the new history of our own time. Fortunately, this function is more than fulfilled by Pushpa Bhave's paper, 'History: Old and New'. The key to the character of her comprehensive coverage is contained in the very first sentence, "We must remind ourselves that history is a way of organizing social reality, which was created by humans and modified by humans over time in particular places.... The writing of history like any social endeavour is embedded in an historical and cultural milieu and must be seen as socially constructed reality." Originating as a discipline in the Western world around Enlightenment, history served the purpose of socializing gentlemanly youth into liberal vision till the middle of the 19th century, when an evolutionary paradigm established the idea of scientific history with centrality of reason as the sole criteria of human conduct. This phase ended in about the 1960s, when a faint figuring of 'new history' in the form of a focus on non-elite groups becomes visible. Significantly influenced by social science concepts and methods, new history was born with the Annales School that championed *'la longue duree'* or a long time span so as to focus on 'glacial but unseen forces moving history in almost imperceptible ways'. The representative work in this regard is that of Braudel, who brought the sciences of geography, ecology, and demography into the domain of history, preparing, in the process, a transnational perspective. Dealing a death blow to the time-worn model of politico-biographic narrative, the Annales School's history introduced a three-tiered hierarchy in historical causation with religion, polity, and culture as mere results arising from the operation of economic and demographic factors. There was a call for 'history without people', one where time stood still. Among the influences from social science, the most fruitful proved that of Max Weber, who offered an alternative to

Marxist economic determinism. In the Weberian approach to research, the historian was advised to transcend her time and place to the best of her capacity so as to draw details from sources of the past as also their meaning in their respective places and times. Moving next to Michel Foucault's impact on 'new social history', Bhave points out its common characteristics, despite the diversity in its methods and assumptions. Quanto-history, psychohistory, and prospography as techniques of research in new social history follow thereafter, as also their critiques. Among the thriving wings of new history are mentioned the Marxists, the Mentalite, and Gender historians. This meticulous macro-level march of history old to history new terminates with major points of criticism such as its deterministic tendency; inaccessibility to the general public; lack of coherence leading to the problem of teaching its content at the school level; its near-total dependence on social science methods and obsession with locating patterns and structures, coupled with consistent indifference to human concerns. Bhave pleads for integration of new history with the old, with methodological diversity and ideological pluralism bringing about fruitful interaction between history and the social sciences. This rather hurried survey of a very competent and complete coverage of the chequered career of history from the formulation of its first principles to the reformulation of its postmodern paradigm from the pen of a litterateur reminds us of the lament of Marwick about the indifference of historians to the nature and basic principles of historical study. He categorically observed, "These things are more discussed by philosophers than by historians ... the philosophers are much readier to say what the historians ought to be doing than the historians are to say what they are doing."[2]

Guided by this ground reality of our subject, we invited a non-historian to present the keynote at our seminar. Also a member from the literati and naturally self-conscious about the central role he had been assigned, Aniket Jaaware subjected the state of the discipline to searching questions and serious analysis so as to sensitize its practitioners to the perception of people outside the discipline. To begin with, he differentiates between two types of 'naïve' historiography, one which reduces the past to names, dates, and numbers, refusing to recognize its presence in the present, and the other which forgets the fact that the past is dead and gone, making us believe that everything in the present is a form of the past. No, Jaaware is in no way contradicting himself, as will be clear from the arguments and examples he marshals to bring home this seemingly irreconcilable simultaneous existence of two kinds naïve historiography: "What is naïve about them is that they do not possess or care to possess any notion of time and the relations between the past, the present, and the future. Our understanding of time is crucial for our view of history as such." Next he proceeds to parody the prevalent modes of verifying historical facts and the principal methods of establishing causation, which constitutes a cornerstone in the structure of historical narrative. By and large, most history books are used to authenticate other books of history and one is lost in a deluge of documents from which fishing out an empirical fact is an impossible feat. If awareness of the time dimension is fundamental to any reconstruction of the past, no less is it so in relation to language, which imposes its own imperatives on the historian. The vanishing line between historical fact and literary fiction should set historians to thinking about their models and methods. More so in the face of carping critique of 'enlightenment rationality' by Michel Foucault. The Annales School's attempt at documenting the history of emotions would require a departure from conventional modes of collecting the data. Jaaware ends his thought-provoking essay with the issue of social memory, which operates every time the past revisits us. Thus, if the preceding piece focused on the past of recording the past, this one brings home to us the relevance of its recording in the present.

From its very genesis as a modern discipline, history has been shaped almost exclusively within Western civilization and this naturally resulted in treating the West as 'self' and reading the non-Western past in terms of 'the other'. Seen against the background of four hundred years of colonization and domination of this 'other' by the West, the rise of the Orientalist approach for rewriting the history of the Orient is understandable. This model may have some similarity with the postcolonial model, but the two are hardly identical. A critical evaluation of the nature, content and methodology of Western historiography of the Orient was inaugurated by Edward W. Said with his epoch-making work, *Orientalism*. In view of the ongoing contemporary discussion on the subject, Raja Dixit was requested to encapsulate and simplify the major issues involved in the various dimensions of the debate. Dixit begins by defining the terminology and tracing the origins of Orientalism in the Indian context. Switching thereafter to Said's thesis, he discusses the four concepts involved, highlighting at the end how, 'because of Orientalism, the orient was not (and is not) a free subject of thought and action'. The all-embracing hold of the ideology is reflected in the fact that we have a 'linguistic Orient, a Freudian Orient, a Spenglerian Orient, a Darwinian Orient, a racist Orient.... There has never been a thing as a pure or unconditional Orient'. In view of the fact that the paper was meant for the Indian student and teacher community, Dixit has given larger coverage to the application of this approach to Indian historiography. His was hardly an easy task and yet he has done it quite competently.

The Marxist model of history is as important in the world context as the Indian. For any course in historiography, a study of the Marxist approach must involve complete understanding of Marxist concepts before undertaking their application in a given historiography. That is what Chhaya Goswami has done and, as expected, she has incorporated a bird's-eye view of the Indian scenario in all three periods of Indian history. Vast indeed is the literature on Marx and the Marxist approach to history and voluminous is the Marxist historiography on India and the article, therefore, naturally attempts a summary of the salient facts and features.

We have seen in Bhave's survey that the movement towards the birth of new history is marked by the milestone of the Annales School, which advocated an all-encompassing study of the past instead of adhering to political and diplomatic developments. History has not looked back ever since and all subsequent models and methods are merely offshoots of the Annales School in some form or the other because the philosophy of the Annales historians was to capture the totality and inner organic unity of the society of any historical period. Aravind Ganachari highlights the central feature of this philosophy with reference to Marc Bloch, who "saw life as a whole, as a complicated interplay of ideals and realities, of conscious innovation and unconscious conservation. Similar to life, history was a whole, that no period and no topic could be understood except in relation to other periods and topics." He discusses Braudel's work in detail, offering an appropriate background to the birth of the school and closes with its critique.

Of all the models and methods of doing history, the most difficult for a historian is, perhaps, the structural one, and for obvious reasons. While history is concerned with facts, its structural model is concerned with the complex web of relations between groupings of facts. Historical investigation is a diachronic study, while the structural approach postulates a synchronic study. The corpus of facts in history is arranged on the principle of compartmentalization, to which the structuralist would be totally opposed. Given this binary opposition between the historical and structural approaches to the study of society, the very idea of their combination carries a clear contradiction. Jatin Wagle attempts this tough task in his paper, 'Structure and Discourse: Reading the Political Unconscious of History', and in spite of conscious efforts, succeeds only to some extent in simplifying the Althusserian modification of the Marxist theory of infrastructure/superstructure and the Jamesanian critique of Foucault's formulation in which history becomes a form of mind among many others. Wagle has left little to desire in explicating the concepts and processes involved in viewing the past in terms of structures and, yet, we feel students of history will find his essay much above their level of understanding.

If the structural approach to a perspective on the past is a little problematic for students of history, no less so is the gender approach. Gender history is normally equated with women's history, which is hardly the case. Few scholars correctly comprehend the application of gender as a category of historical investigation. "Gender history starts with the distinction made between gender and sex, in that gender adds to sex expectations of cultural propriety and power relationships. These are made and not given and they have a maker as well as receiver." Fortunately for us, a social scientist of international repute accepted the task of penning the paradigm and parameters of gender history in so concise and clear a manner as to be easily accessible to students. 'History through the Gender Lens' by Maithreyi Krishnaraj thoroughly investigates the field, offering a feminist critique of available historiography as also Krishnaraj's own reservations about some methods and assumptions of feminist approach to history. This shows that if her concern is genuine in demanding due place for women in history, it is hardly less so in upholding the healthy principles of historical investigation.

The purpose of most postcolonial histories could legitimately be correcting the colonial assumptions about the past of the people concerned, aiming to author an authentic account in which the colonial 'other' becomes the postcolonial 'self'. However, in postcolonial Indian historiography, a school of historians rejected, not only imperial accounts of nationalist struggle, but those of nationalists as well, terming both as elitist in content and hegemonic in nature. Inspired by the ideas of Italian Marxist Antonio Gramsci, this group comes to be called 'subaltern' after the hero of history it intended documenting. Radhika Seshan's paper is concerned with the birth and growth of subaltern historiography in terms of its origin, nature, features, literature, and a critique.

If the job of Jatin Wagle was termed tough in explicating the structural approach, that of C.R. Das was much more so in concretizing the nebulous nature of the postmodern critique of conventional historiography. Ridding the attempt of attendant rhetoric was not easy to accomplish and, yet, Das has succeeded in weaving the salient features of postmodern *problematique* into a system where none appears to exist. Das is obliged to use tough technical terms like 'de-differentiation' and 'deterritorialization', but offers their meanings immediately in brackets so as to ease an otherwise arduous exercise. The relevance of the postmodern perspective on the past is reflected in the fact that history is regarded as a cornerstone in the structure of modernity. "The emergence and growth of history as a discipline has much to do with the entire epistemology that the enlightenment modernity produced, with its thrust on the notion of 'scientific' as incorporated in the philosophy and methodology of empiricist, rationalist, and positivist scientific epistemology and enquiry." Even while admitting the failure of postmodernism to produce any alternative system in the opening paragraph of his article, Das has identified and enumerated no less than twelve issues that emerge from the postmodern critique of history. His select bibliography at the end would further help the student in developing a deeper understanding of the fast-growing phenomenon.

Finally, regional history in relation to India has its own special relevance in view of its subcontinental size and wide variations in topography, climate, and environment. The concept and its application, however, are not as simple as they might appear. Region as a unit of history is difficult to define. The colonial historians attempted documenting the history of certain communities originating in or inhabiting particular pieces of Indian geography, but the end products could hardly be termed as examples of regional history. The last article of this anthology, therefore, is devoted to discussing the principles and practice of regional history with their attendant issues. With very little theorization being done, Umesh Kadam had to base his article on scattered and incidental references. If this enhances the value of his brief essay on the one hand, it also indicates the research potential of the field on the other.

Having contextualized each paper[3] of our collection and briefly bringing out its content and contribution, we can legitimately claim that it will more than meet the needs of students and teachers in grappling with the growing variety of perspectives on the past. This plurality of historical perspective emanating from diverse directions obliged the UGC to restructure and redesign courses in historiography. If it was befitting to open our Introduction with the opening sentence of the UGC curriculum, it will be equally so now to end with an idea of the emerging scenario in its own words: "History like other disciplines is a growing subject and perspectives and interpretations tend to change with new theories, influence of other disciplines, new methods of analysis availability of new sources, and changing contexts. There is an ongoing debate on various historical issues. Is history essentially a narrative of events or is it concerned with structures? How securely based is our knowledge of the past? Can history be objective? Answers to such questions have been widely divergent and have occasioned intense debates over the years."[4] We hardly need to point out the utility of the papers we have put together in sensitizing and familiarizing the student with the vast and varied domain described above by the UGC Committee on Model Curriculum in History and Archaeology.

Notes

1. UGC Model Curriculum, *History and Archaeology*, University Grants Commission, New Delhi, 2001, p.1.
2. Arthur Marwick, *The Nature of History*, Macmillan, Reprint, Chennai, 1976, p.9.
3. We need to clarify a glaring discrepancy arising from a few papers with footnotes and most papers without footnotes. The collection in origin represents the partial proceedings of the seminar we organised to generate basic reading material in the form of a textbook, in which each chapter on the given theme would contain at the end a list of books for further reading. There was, therefore, no necessity of footnotes as the papers were not expected to be research papers. But a few contributors felt the need, while the paper of Pushpa Bhave had an origin outside the seminar.
4. UGC Model Curriculum, op. cit., p.1.

1

History

Old and New

Pushpa Bhave

Before looking at the movements in new history, we must first remind ourselves that history is a way of organizing social reality which was created by humans and modified by humans over time in particular places. Therefore, a set of questions we must always keep in mind is who wrote history, in what age was it written, and in what cultural context and under what circumstances were its categories formed? We especially need to be mindful of history in our own age and why certain people chose certain models and interpretations and which individuals or groups benefit from the interpretations chosen. The writing of history, like any social endeavour, is embedded in a historical and cultural milieu and must be seen as a socially constructed reality.

We must further remind ourselves that history as a discipline and a profession has been shaped almost exclusively within Western civilization, particularly Western culture, since the Enlightenment. No major historical paradigm, which now has currency, has come from outside the Western world. In India, the field of subaltern studies is largely a variation of Marxist studies and the new history of France and England. Perhaps, not coincidentally, it was during the rise of the West, during 1600-1950, that most major historical models were developed and many of these still dominate the field.

Among European historians from the 16th until well into the 19th century, history was the domain of the gentlemanly tradition of high culture. Often, this elite group used history to justify the power relations within their own societies and the primacy of their own nation in the larger world. History to these gentlemen amateurs was an exercise in moral instruction, which proved that God's will and human virtue triumphed in the world. In turn, this morally determined history served the purpose of socializing youth to the liberal vision. History made up an important element in the school curriculum to bring each new generation into the system and to train leaders who would be confident in their own future exercise of power.

This type of morally determined history, often called Whig history,[1] was challenged in the late 19th century by the rise of the first professional historians. Between 1870 and 1930, history became a separate profession and universities established history departments, which offered PhDs in history. Professional historical societies were founded such as the American Historical Association in 1887.

The concept of social change, which animated this history, was the newly discovered process of evolution. The idea of an objective scientific history can be traced to modern Europe, where science had gained legitimacy among intellectuals in the 19th century. In the search for these social laws, the metaphor of biologism or mechanism almost always underlay the models. This approach saw human life in groups as governed by the same principles as biological life. Hence, systems of human relations, historical movement, and historical causation could be isolated, identified, and analysed as could a blood, digestive, or neurological system in the human body. The reign of scientific history was brief, lasting only from about 1870 till 1940.

The new concept of evolution served to demonstrate how human institutions evolved finally into liberal nation states. The agenda for historical research was largely political, administrative and constitutional change in these nation states. The relations among these states provided another significant area for the new professional history. Historians described political and administrative events, great and small, in minute detail, usually without trying to relate these political events to the larger historical context of their time and place. The majority of the articles published in the new historical journals such as *The English Historical Review, American Historical Review*, and the *Revue Historique*, between 1920 and 1955, were devoted to this approach and to these topics. Most historians of this period wrote as one new history critic has alleged, "as if Freud or Nietzsche had never lived, so that the men they wrote about were not only wholly rational, but also rational in certain very limited ways – *homo economicus* or *homo politicus* or *homo theologicus* ..."[2]

A minority of the professional historians during this period was searching for small or grand theories to explain history, but they did not have great influence on the profession itself. Visionaries like Spengler or Toynbee had their own models for the rise and fall of civilizations, but only a few devotees and readers in the general public kept this movement alive in an age which honoured fragmentation of human experience rather than any larger synthesis.

However, in the 1960s, many of the younger historians in the profession began to challenge, not only the choice of groups studied by their mentors in older political history, but also the methods the older generation used. By the 1970s, this trickle of challenges to the old way of doing history had merged into a flood of revisionism, which collectively became known as new history or sometimes new social history. What the approaches of new history had in common was more of what they were against than any real consensus on what new history actually was. For the most part, new history departed radically from the earlier histories of the evolutionary and economically determined narratives of the first hundred years of professional history. Moreover, the new historians eschewed the older historians' concern for politics, diplomacy, and constitutionalism. New history all but put an end to these areas of research. An even more radical departure from the earlier focus of history is apparent in new history's fascination with any group as long as that group could not be considered an 'elite' in economic, political, or any other form of power.

New history is far more inclusive of the diverse and neglected groups of people than the old history was. Through new history's doors have entered into historical consciousness for the first time slaves, peasants, workers, women, children, and numerous other groups that have made up the vast majority of people who have ever lived on this planet. They have entered conscious history, not as in the past as objects of some more powerful elite, but as subjects and agents of their own history. At the same time, the concerns and questions of new history have expanded in all directions away from the older, political and diplomatic story of nation-states and their leaders to focus on exciting new areas of human activity such as death, sex, nutrition, disease, community, cosmologies, and, most of all, human associations and human meanings.

A major factor in the increased influence of new history is the social background of historians since 1945 and their tendency to be identified with radical causes and their sympathy with the exploited peoples of the world. In many areas, new immigrants, persons from lower social classes, women, and people from non-professional families are entering the scholarly professions, particularly the new social sciences. Individuals coming from these backgrounds quite naturally bring to the history and social science professions new perspectives based on their own experiences as minorities, women, and members of the lower class. Often, scholars with non-elite backgrounds are somewhat ill at ease in the heretofore privileged ranks of the university educated and this alienation sometimes translates into a heightened social conscience. At the same time, the number and influence of professional historians in the non-Western world has grown dramatically and their understandable disenchantment with the dominant liberal or Whig view of history has motivated many to seek out approaches and groups to study which can provide an alternate view to the colonial history they learned in school. In addition to the more socially concerned ideology of the new social historians around the world, they have introduced many new topics for study, most of which are related to their own concerns and identity as peasants, poor, lower caste, women, and workers – in brief, the concerns of the more exploited and voiceless groups.

New history has been significantly influenced by social-science concepts and methods as well as the changing nature of Western societies and the erosion of Western dominance in the world. From the social sciences, the new historians have liberally borrowed concepts such as social structure, role theory, kinship, and mentalities or meanings. Among the fast-changing political arrangements in the world since 1945, certainly the end of colonialism and the subsequent rise of new nations around the world have been significant factors in shaping new history. Within many societies, the voice and political power of mass movements has meant a greater appreciation and empathy for hitherto voiceless communities whose stories lie buried in the past.

In searching for the roots of new history, most historians look to France and to the founding of the Annales School by Marc Bloch in 1929. The political and diplomatic historians in the late 1920s dominated the field in France. The journal *The Annales d'Histoire: Economique et Social*, later renamed *Annales, Economies, Societies, Civilizations*, founded in 1929, was begun to oppose the political and diplomatic historians whom the Annalists derisively labelled the Sorbonnistes.[3]

One of the key concepts in the Annales approach to history is *la longue duree*, or the long term, the belief that glacial, but unseen forces are moving history in almost imperceptible ways. Certainly, two of the formative influences on the geology of history approach have been Fernand Braudel and

Marc Bloch. Ironically, the fall of France and even the subsequent imprisonment of Braudel only reinforced their belief in gradual change shaped by impersonal forces. In his recollection of the fall of France in 1940, Bloch referred to his colleagues as

> either specialists in the social sciences or workers in scientific laboratories, and may be the very disciplines of those employments kept us, by a sort of fatalism, from embarking on individual action. We had grown used to seeing great impersonal forces at work in society as in nature. In the vast drag of these submarine swells, so cosmic as to seem irresistible, of what avail were the petty struggles of a few shipwrecked sailors. To think otherwise would have been to falsify history.[4]

While serving in prison during the German occupation of France, Braudel completed his first version of *The Mediterranean and the Mediterranean World in the Age of Philip II.* Braudel's landmark book championed '*la longue duree*' and the '*inanimate*' forces of geography, demography, and economy that were the deeper realities of history. Compared with these forces, 'the passions of Philip II and the ideas of the Renaissance were cockleshells tossed on the waters of history'.[5&6] Braudel has said of his times:

> All those occurrences which poured in upon us from the radio and the newspapers of our enemies, or even the news from London ... I had to outdistance, reject, deny them. Down with occurrences, especially vexing ones! I had to believe that history, destiny, was written at a much more profound level.[7]

Braudel concludes his *Mediterranean* by opting for the triumph of the long term over individuals doomed to live in the short term:

> So when I think of the individual, I am always inclined to see him imprisoned within a destiny in which he himself has little hand, fixed in a landscape in which the infinite perspectives of the long term stretch into the distance both behind him and before. In historical analysis, as I see it, rightly or wrongly, the

> long term always wins in the end... it indubitably limits both the freedom of the individual and even the role of chance.[8]

Braudel's monumental work has been one of the most significant influences on new history since World War II. It was one of the first successful attempts to employ social science approaches to writing history. Braudel stresses geography, ecology, and demography as the major factors which established the limits of human action. He has also introduced a transnational perspective and brings into the context not only France and its history, but Ottoman Islam, Latin Christianity, and other groups surrounding the Mediterranean basin. All of these strands come together in the Battle of Lepanto in 1571. In the context of malaria epidemics, overcutting of trees, soil exhaustion, the cycle of population rise and decline, and economic fluctuations, the free will actions of even key actors such as Phillip II, to Braudel, seem only marginally important in the shaping of the societies in the Mediterranean world. Following the major impact of the *The Mediterranean and The Mediterranean World*, many of Braudel's Annales followers adopted this kind of ecological-technical-demographic-geographic determinism. This approach still characterizes some of the best French history writing.

The French historians of the Annales School have been particularly harsh on the narrative and political versions of history. To them, history, which treats events and contingencies or what they term *histoire evenementielle*, rather than deep structures and long-term patterns, is mere chronology and gossip. Jacques Le Goff, of the *Ecole Pratique des Hautes Etudes*, has explained that

> the Annales School loathed .... political history, narrative history, and chronicle or episodic history. All of these for them was mere pseudo history, history on the cheap, a superficial affair which preferred the shadow to the substance. What had to be put in its place was history in depth – an economic, social, and mental history.

He went on to call "the old political history dead but not yet buried, a corpse that has to be made to lie down".[9]

> Beyond their distaste for narrative history, the Annales historians took the lead in developing a theory for the new history. The theory owed much to geology and geography as metaphors and offered a three-tiered hierarchy to explain historical causation. At the base of social movement, and the most important elements, are the economic and demographic factors (the geology of history). Then comes social structure and lastly there is the intellectual, religious, political, and cultural factors, which are seen as mere results of the more basic engines of social change.

The French '*la longue duree*' or long-term, unlike Marxist history,[10] hardly moves at all. The surface movement of politics, according to them, is the mere illusion of change. Deep down underneath this surface, the base factors move at the pace of a glacier, or not at all. "The muse of history herself nowadays disdains," according to Emmanual Le Roy-Ladurie, one of the most talented of the newer Annales historians, "those long sequences of simple and uncomplicated events so beloved of historians of the old school."[11] If only the material conditions of the masses constituted real change, Ladurie and the other advocates of the long-term history argue, "nothing, absolutely nothing, changed over the five centuries from the 14th to the 18th centuries in continental Europe."[12]

This long-term history sees nothing worth mentioning in such trivial movements or events as the Renaissance, Reformation, the Enlightenment or even the rise of national states. Rather, history of the long term sees only an immobile history, where the demographic and economic realities of the masses did not change at all. Le Roy-Ladurie has even called for a 'history without people', or a kind of history where time stands still.[13]

The Annales School's early base was predominantly economic and social history. However, in recent years, it has added to these approaches aspects of anthropology, sociology, demography, geography, psychology, and semiotics. The battle between the old history of politics and the new history championed by the Annales School was a long and bitter struggle.

Under the significant influence of the rich variety of new approaches of the Annales School, historians in other nations began to seek new ways of understanding history and since 1945, these efforts have culminated in the new history, largely a creation of Western historians and social scientists. These developments in new history have, especially since the 1960s, come mostly from France, England, and the United States where there are large, professional groups of historians. Their writings have been collectively labelled the 'new social history'.[14]

The single greatest influence on the development of the new social history comes from the social sciences. Following the Annales lead, the new historians nearly always select their conceptual models, their methodologies, and their questions from the social science disciplines. Within the influences from social science, none has been more important to historians than the discovery of the German historical sociologist, Max Weber (1864-1920). According to one of the premier American new historians, the translation of Max Weber in the 1950s:

> probably did more to influence the writing of history in the 1960s than any other single influence from the social sciences, particularly since he offered an alternative to vulgar Marxist economic determinism, which was by then falling into historical disrepute; to Marxist theories of class, which were by then appearing to be largely inapplicable to pre-modern societies; and to vulgar Marxist theories of change in the means of production as the prime generating force for change in other aspects of society.[15]

The impact of the Weberian assumptions was particularly significant in the United States, where professional historians had been, for most of the 20th century, under the spell of one form or another of economic determinism and also of evolution. Beginning in the 1960s, more and more American historians began to accept with Weber that institutional, ideological, and especially cultural factors were not mere products of an assumed economic base, but had themselves significant power in the making of history. By the 1970s, even American historians, who studied their own past, were beginning to see cultural influence in a new way. In 1978, Robert Kelly, a California historian, wrote an article in *The New York Times*, in which he announced that:

> A new way of seeing American politics is emerging among historians. For generations, they described political history as the product of economic forces, that is, class conflict and geographic factors. Now they see cultural politics at work: Irishmen against Englishmen, Chicanos against Wasps, moralists against free thinkers, blacks against whites, Catholics against Protestants, teetotallers against drinkers, and Yankees against white Southerners. Ethnic identity, religion, styles of life – these figure prominently in the new histories, and they have given us a strikingly new picture of the American past.[16]

Even before the Weberian influence stressing cultural factors in human history became acceptable, Western historians, excluding the older Marxists, were usually faithful to Weber's philosophy of method. Weber had separated the morality of truth from the morality of what he termed responsibility. Weber saw science and the objective search for truth as a value that which historians must accept as a foundation of their vocation. Weber's value of pursuing truth is quite different from a concept of truth as something which can be scientifically validated once and for all. Trying to be truthful is not the same as possessing the truth. The Weberian approach to research means that the historian tries to transcend his own time and place and attempts, to the best of his capacity, to ferret out the details and their meaning for other times and places, always being faithful to the available sources and the rules of evidence. The political or social consequences of this search are supposed to be secondary to the actual objective stance of the researcher. The anthropologist, Clifford Geertz, one of the gurus of new history, uses the image of a hospital operating room: It is supposed to be germ free, but we can never totally achieve that objective. The implication of this failure, however, does not mean it would be better to perform surgery in a sewer.

Historians face the paradox of living in a particular time and culture and holding personal and social values, and yet trying to free themselves from that parochialism in order to study other times and places. Weber also offered a way out of that dilemma. He advised us to take a current concern or value and turn it into a question for the past. We could research about freedom, alienation, class conflict, gender issues, or other burning topics of our time in other times and places if we were careful to ask questions within the frames of discourse of that other time and place. Are we reading the present backward when we do this? To a certain extent, that must happen. Can asking our questions of the past illuminate the past? Many historians think so. This approach and method is central to new social history. Even though the questions are framed in our own time, historians seek to find answers that emerge by hearing the voices of the past in their own cadence. Neo-Marxist scholars in Europe and the United States also accept this historiography rooted in respect for evidence.

Beyond the recent influence of Weber, a still continuing influence is that of Karl Marx and Friedrich Engels. However, the new Marxist historians have drastically changed some of the assumptions of Marx himself and many have adapted methods and approaches from Weber and other sociologists. Most of them also rely on the conventional rules of evidence shared by other historians in demonstrating the validity of their research.

Michel Foucault has also become a major philosopher in shaping the questions and approaches of the new social history. Foucault, a current cult figure in social science and history, tells us that our categories are related to power and the desire to control others or to maintain social control. Therefore, we must always ask when new categories such as sexual dysfunction, madness, and deviancy come into the discourse and for what purpose these concepts are socialized.

Louis Dumont, like Foucault, a fellow Frenchman and a major figure in cognitive anthropology, has spent much of his life in India. Dumont argues that our concepts of the human self are also historical and socially created products. Dumont maintains that the individualized economic man is a product of modern Europe and he argues that the individualized self is also a product of modern European history.

Peter Berger's concept of the social construction of reality is a cogent summary of how most social historians imagine that reality is produced. Berger explains in his *Social Construction of Reality*:

> How is it possible that subjective meanings become objective facticities? Or, how is it possible that human activity should produce a world of things? In other words, an adequate understanding of the '*reality sui generis*' of society requires an inquiry into the manner in which this reality is constructed.[17]

The impact of social science on the new history is readily apparent when the major topics of study are assembled from indices to current historical journals and to papers presented at conferences of historical associations. New American journals, such as *Comparative Studies in Society and History*, the *Journal of Interdisciplinary History*, the *Journal of Social History*, *Computers and the Humanities*, *The History of Childhood Quarterly*, *Journal of Psycho-History* and *Family History*, all convey the enormous influence of social science on the writing of new history. Clearly, the categories of assumptions and methods of new history are not just coincidentally similar to the concerns of the social sciences. In the major historical studies of the past twenty years, familiar concepts from social science are now the major guides to historical research as well.

Categories such as childhood, adolescence, madness, homosexuality, and feminine and deviant behaviour have all been analysed in their historical context to determine what purpose each served and how and why these concepts came into existence. The new social history often focuses on the local community, kinship and family, personal attitudes, and collective meanings, all these being areas of traditional social science research.

Edward Shils, one of the most influential social scientists in the Western world, who teaches at the universities of both Chicago and Cambridge, says of this merger of social science and history:

> We are seeing in the United States the first signs of an amalgamation of history and the social sciences .... The outcome, which we can see at present only in a very incipient state, is a scholarly comparative social science and a comparative history. It is the beginning of a true 'science humaine'.[18]

The new history, even though diverse in its methods and assumptions, has several characteristics in common. It eschews narrative history and up until the recent influence of anthropology, seeks to write analytical history. Almost all of the major historical works done in the last twenty years are analytical rather than narrative. The new social history also stresses the why of history and the ensuing consequences, rather than the what and how of the older history. The new history also focuses on different dimensions of human life as the old history did not.

The first major area of attention on which the new historians initially focused was the material basis of human life. This category includes the limits caused by demographic shifts, human geography and ecology, the levels of technology and the type of economic system. These areas were first opened up by the French Annalistes. A second major area of focus was the whole range of institutions below the nation-state level. These levels included the systems of distribution of wealth, status and power; socialization agencies such as schools and families; social control agencies such as prisons, asylums, and the police; institutions of work such as business firms and unions; institutions for government such as town meetings, political machines and caste associations, and institutions for leisure such as museums, festivals, and sports. Within these institutions, the new historians look for social processes such as class mobility, changing distributions of power, wealth and status, conflict and cooperation among and between groups, and the roots of social movements, whether in religion, mass movements, elites, or other realms of consciousness formation.

A third major focus of the new history is in the cultural-social history of image making in the collective consciousness. This focus looks at opinion formation, the relationship of popular culture and politics, and, most importantly, the formation of culture among illiterate groups. This field has become one of the fastest growing areas of the new history and is strongly influenced by cultural anthropology and its interest in meaning and conceptual systems of category formation.

The field of urban history is not entirely a new field, however, the way new historians approach the study of cities has changed dramatically from the older studies. The new history has spawned a large number of studies of old and newer cities and of small towns as well. The newer approaches taken to the study of urban history range widely from demographics[19] and religious values[20] to new approaches to urban politics.[21]

The history of the family has also gained greatly as a new field for social history. The new approach to family history emphasizes kinship ties, family structures, changing sex roles, changing attitudes toward sexuality, and ties between husbands and wives, parents and children.[22]

Beyond these areas of focus, the interests of the new social history have coalesced around several major fields of history and method. Demographic history was one of the first fields to develop into a strong sub-group of new history. This field lent itself readily to the sophisticated computers which first became available in the 1960s. The computer and other mathematical tools have enabled historians to arrange and make sense of vast amounts of census data, parish records of birth, marriage and deaths, and other unexplored statistical accounts. These small-scale, but intensive, studies have added important new information, which indicate important trends over long periods. For example, since the 16th century in North America and Western Europe, there has been a trend towards late marriages and low fertility. Some of the best works of this type have been written by French historians of the Annales School. Le Roy-Ladurie, working with a team, was able to computerize 78 variables for 3,000 districts from the French census for the period from 1819 to 1930. Another team of Americans, led by Theodore Hershberg, is analysing some 2.5 million people covered in the Philadelphia census from 1850 to 1880.[23]

Another important research technique is to separate the larger civilization into a small manageable unit, which lends itself to a total analysis in the manner of anthropologists. This approach led to local history, the in-depth study of a community, a village, or sometimes a province. The best of the works are by French scholars such as Pierre Boubert and Le Roy-Ladurie for provinces, Pierre Deyon for a city, and Martine Segalen and Gerard Bouchard for a village. American colonial history has also employed this type of study with Kenneth Lockridge's study of Lynn, Massachusetts, and John Demos' study of a Plymouth plantation. Certainly, the classic study in this type is Le Roy-Ladurie's study of a century French village, Montaillou. This book has become a bestseller in France and a classic throughout the world of history, even though it is not narrative history and tells no story. Rather, Le Roy-Ladurie takes us on an unforgettable journey, which meanders inside the villagers' heads.[24]

The focus on small units of analysis like town, village, or community brings with it an attention to very different populations in those units as well. The new historians look at average people in their small locales. This new emphasis was eloquently phrased by the eminent French historian, Le Roy-Ladurie:

> From Rocroi to Crulai; from Waterloo to Colyton – these four place-names could be said to sum up the course taken over the past hundred and fifty years by a certain school of history, from the resounding, action-packed historiography of the 19th century, battle-history, to the silent, mathematical resurrection of a total past represented today in historical demography. Crulai and Colyton, obscure little villages in Normandy and Devon, certainly have none of the echoing notoriety of the victories (or defeats) of Rocro and Waterloo, nor have the learned works inspired by these tiny peasant communities appeared in massive editions or provided scenarios for films or bestsellers .... And yet it is thanks to these villages and to a few others; thanks to the parish registers of Crulai, Colyton, Auneuil, Saint-Lambert-des-Levees, etc.... that the decisive techniques of family reconstruction were first developed, then tested .... Without flourish of trumpets, these techniques have shed new light on past societies ...[25]

As Le Roy-Ladurie's statement suggests, the average people in these small towns is the real stuff of history. Gone are the mayors, bankers, kings, and emperors, replaced by the heretofore silent masses of the past. The concern with average people as a major way of looking at history is shared by most of the new historians. In this effort they are attempting to bring to consciousness the histories of the vast majority of people who have lived, but whose thoughts, ways of life, and view of the universe historians have not up to now charted or analysed. There has been a deliberate attempt by the new historians to turn from their fascination with past holders of political, cultural, and economic power toward the inarticulate masses of the past. Beyond the numerous works on small towns and villages, other new historians have searched for and presented us with new forms of group consciousness: Eugene Genovese has explored the consciousness of slaves, E.P. Thompson and Eric Hobsbawm, the English working class, Georges Lefebvre and Emmanuel Le Roy-Ladurie, the French peasantry, Natalie Davis and Gerda Lerner, women, and Philip Aries, children.

The American historian, Lawrence Stone, chairman of the Princeton history department and a leading figure in the mentalite school, has divided current historians into four major groups: "... the old narrative historians, primarily political historians and biographers; the cliometricians who continue to act like statistical junkies; the hard-nosed social historians still busy analysing impersonal structures and the historians of mentalite, now chasing ideals, values, mindsets, and patterns of intimate personal behaviour – the more intimate the better."[26]

Another of the important new historians, the Marxist E.J. Hobsbawm, wrote in 1971 that the most interesting social history of the preceding 10-15 years fell under the topics or complexes of questions, including (1) demography and kinship; (2) urban studies insofar as they fall within our field; (3) classes and social groups; (4) the study of 'mentalities' or collective consciousness or of 'culture' in the anthropological sense; (5) the transformation of societies (for example, modernization or industrialization); and (6) social movements and phenomena of social protest. He went on to explain why these fields had become important, suggesting that "scholarship had previously avoided such subjects, because they were implicitly subversive of established institutions and loyalties. Now it turned to them for precisely the same reason. They became a means of understanding the errors of the past and possibilities of the future."[27]

One of the major groups of historians in new social history, and the first to gain legitimacy after 1950, were the cliometricians, so called because of their use of statistical approaches which could be used on the newly invented computers. The cliometricians were the closest of all the new historians in methodology to traditional historians who, particularly in economic history, had used quantification for years.[28] What was unique about the new historical quantifiers was their very scientific approach to method and their application of the method in all phases of history. The cliometricians had to be highly trained in mathematics and statistics. They subjected social, cultural, religious, and biographical history to statistical analysis.

Most of the early cliometric historians were economic historians, but by the 1970s, historians from varied fields had turned toward statistical analysis. David Herlihy, one of the major figures in cliometrics, prophesied in 1981, "The historian of the 1980s may not have to be a programmer, but he will have to know how the computer can assist in all phases of his work. Otherwise, he would be derelict in his duties as a scientist and as a historian."[29]

One of the best efforts at quanto-history was Robert Fogel's and Stanley Engerman's *Time on the Cross*, subtitled, *The Economics of American Negro Slavery*.[30] The unusual format of the book featured a one-volume collection of data and statistics and an additional volume of interpretation. By analysing data on numbers and prices of slaves, numbers of families broken up as a result of sales, average age of black women at the time of the birth of their first child, the authors made generalizations about the sexual mores of blacks and whites, the stability of the black family, the sex roles within the family, and the relations among the races. The overall objective, however, was to establish the degree of profitability of slavery as an institution, which they concluded made slavery a viable economic system.

Despite some innovative approaches to history, cliometrics has suffered from harsh attacks, not only from the older narrative historians, but from the new historians as well. Jacques Barzun in his *Cleo and the Doctors*, assails quanto-history because he thinks it is mechanistic and deterministic, focusing only on one aspect of reality, while reducing all else to that one level. Oscar Handlin's criticism of cliometrics was more subtle. Handlin alleged that quantification methods diverted attention from the more fundamental issues of historical research. Some studies, he suggested, "make modest contributions to the understanding of problems posed by the examination of conventional sources". However, he went on, "quantification at this level involves classifying and counting; and technology makes the task more expeditious, but demands no shifts in conceptualization".[31]

In his presidential address to the Economic History Association in 1977, David Landes, a long-time advocate of quantification techniques, shared his doubts about the assumptions of cliometrics:

> The data of economic history consist in large part of those qualitative, non-quantitative bits that have always been the concern and delight of the conventional historian. The sorting and counting may come later, but someone must find and report the raw material that goes into tables and times series .... Many, if not most, of the important questions that we have to deal with do not lend themselves ... to quantitative treatment.[32]

As the 1980s began, it was clear that cliometrics had not forged to the forefront of new history. In addition, it has such severe limitations as a method that it no longer amounts to anything but another technique, which must be used judiciously. It has failed as a method which would by itself open up any new understanding of the past.

A second major sub-field of new history, which has also come under severe criticism, is psychohistory. Like other models of analysis, the use of psychology in history is not entirely new. Harry Elmer Barnes wrote right after World War I, "The modern psychological historian who accepted the Carlylian interpretation of history will need to revise the famous phrase that history is collective biography to read that history is the record of the collective sublimation of the neuroses and psychoses of the great personalities of history."[33] By 1957, William Langer, a diplomatic historian, who was then president of the American Historical Association, stated in his presidential address that history had been broadened by new fields, but that now 'there was still room for penetration in depth, specifically an urgent need existed to deepen historical understanding through the use of the concepts and findings of modern psychology'. What Langer meant by this was not the use of older psychological approaches, but the methods and concepts of psychoanalysis and in-depth psychology.

Following Langer's lead, several historians moved to explore history through the eyes of psychology. Veteran historians such as H. Stuart Hughes became enthusiastic supporters of the new psychohistory.[34] In the area of group psychology, some attempts have been provocative such as Philippe Aries' *Centuries of Childhood: A Social History of Family Life*[35] and Stanley Elkins' *Slavery: A Problem in American Institutional and Intellectual Life*.[36] For the more common approach of applying the insights of psychoanalysis, the results have been somewhat less valuable.

Bruce Mazlish proved to be one of the most inveterate of the psychohistorians. Mazlish has written, "Psychoanalysis differs from history in one fundamental way. It claims to have a scientific system of concepts, based on clinical data. This claim I accept."[37] His studies have placed on the couch such historical luminaries as John Stuart Mill, Karl Marx and Mao Zedung as well as Richard Nixon, Jimmy Carter and Henry Kissinger. In his studies Mazlish relies almost exclusively on Freudian concepts and sees all of his figures in terms of Oedipal complexes, infantile sexuality, and sublimation of id drives. However, as Mazlish himself freely admits, there simply is not enough data on the childhoods of his subjects to make possible anything but a speculative analysis of their inner drives and psyches.

Certainly, the acknowledged best of the psychohistories comes, not from a professional historian, but from the well-known psychoanalyst, Erik Ericson. His study of Martin Luther is generally regarded as a classic in this field. His work,

Gandhi's Truth, is also considered a significant contribution to psychohistory. However, even Ericson is cautious and has suggested that the term, psychohistory, be used only with 'tacit quotation marks'. Most historians would now probably agree with Oscar Handlin's perceptive evaluation of psychohistory:

> The fundamental mode of analysis (of psychoanalysis) is unavailable to the historian. The patient is not there to answer questions. The process of diagnosis is difficult enough for the skilled therapist, who can ask and listen after passing through a long apprenticeship and analysis, and who, even so, often yields to the impulses to pontificate.[38]

Because of the severe limitations in applying intensive interview techniques with the subject over a period of years to dead people, the methodology of psychoanalysis has not proven very useful in writing history. Furthermore, the dominance of the Freudian model in the West, which has been increasingly attacked for its extreme ethnocentrisms and sexism, creates an inbuilt bias against this type of study. The approach of psychohistory is also profoundly culture bound because of its almost total reliance on Freudian assumptions and, to a lesser extent, the work of Karl Jung, both of whom are products of Western culture. These assumptions, especially the Freudian ones, are increasingly being criticized by Western scholars and even in the field of psychoanalysis itself. Psychology now finds itself dealing with many Freudian assumptions that are unverifiable in any scientific sense. The universality of certain childhood experiences such as birth traumas, weaning traumas, toilet-training traumas, guilt feelings resulting from Oedipal complexes are, as one critic says of them, "we now know to be historically, and probably also theoretically, untrue."[39]

However, certain aspects of psychohistory are still promising. The attempt by Carl Schorske to place the collective psyche, not on the couch, but to see it as operating in the context of the middle-class culture of the late 19th century

Vienna, gives to psychohistory a larger and sounder basis of analysis.[40]

Another social science technique, prosopography, has proven a fruitful technique in the historical research of new history. This line of enquiry stresses career-line analysis, which involves investigating the common characteristic of a group of actors at a particular time in history. Uniform patterns are derived about the group by looking at variables such as death, birth, marriage and family background, social class, inherited position, wealth and source of wealth, religious affiliation, political ideology, etc. One of the most ambitious attempts using this method was Lawrence Stone's collecting biography of the English aristocracy.

The focus of Stone's analysis was a huge catalogue of four samples of country houses and those who had owned them over the centuries. What he garnered from the study was 'a reliable body of statistical evidence', which would 'supplant the subjective impressions and traditional assumptions' that had been handed down.[41]

The two major wings of new history, the Marxist and mentalite schools have both survived and prospered in the 1970s and 1980s and they remain the most innovative and productive schools of the movement. The Marxist historians, increasingly powerful in history departments all over the world, are no longer working in academic isolation, but are becoming increasingly integrated in the mainstream of historical studies. The new cultural historians, one of the most exciting and newest tracks of new history, has been strongly influenced by cultural anthropology. This mentalite history, as it is popularly known, owes much of its inspiration to the semiotic anthropologists, particularly Mary Douglas, Clifford Geertz, and Victor Turner. A third thriving group in new history consists of those interested in gender. At the 1987 annual meeting of the American Historical Association, the largest number of panels on any single topic dealt with gender issues. In this field of new history, the voices are swelling into a genuine mass movement and the nature of the critiques issuing from women's history is perhaps the most potentially re-orienting of the many paradigms and new directions that are being suggested by the new historians. Since these three areas are now the most significant sub-fields of new history, each will be dealt as a classic of this field.

Triumph of New History

By 1976, the new historians of the Annales School had become the elite historians in France. Soon after, in the United States, the new historians had routed all but a few of the older narrative historians from the field. In England, new history came to prominence with the ascendancy of the journal, *Past and Present*, and by the 1980s the new social history, particularly of the Marxist variety, had supplanted the old history there as well. In American colleges and universities, courses in political history have decreased dramatically since World War II and the number of courses on social history have increased correspondingly.[42]

Under the new social history, narrative history, the mainstay of older historical writing, became a thing of the past. Le Roy-Ladurie attacked the old history and confidently explained in 1973 that "present-day historiography, with its preference for the quantifiable, the statistical and the structural, has been obliged to suppress (old narrative history) in order to survive... in the last few decades". He contends, "It has virtually condemned to death the narrative history of events and the individual biography."[43]

Narrative histories concerned with events and people, Le Roy-Ladurie suggested, survive today only because of 'cultural supermarkets' and the effect of mass media. Le Roy-Ladurie was confident that history had now come to give up the 'long sequences of simple and uncomplicated events' that characterized the old narrative history and now, at last, historians were concerned with structures and patterns of the long term and assembling data which could prove, through quantitative analysis, the legitimacy of these patterns. "Anything which might impede this movement," he warns, "would be crushed."[44]

A glance at the indices of major historical journals in the past few years amply confirms Le Roy-Ladurie's prediction on the triumph of new history. The December 1985 *American Historical Review* carried articles such as 'Popular Unrest in Paris from 1557-1572', 'Vagrants, Beggars and Bandits in Cuba from 1878-1895'; 'The Stature and Nutrition in the Hapsburg Monarchy in the Eighteenth Century'. The April 1986 issue carried articles on 'Cotton Mill People: Work, Community and Protest in the Textile South, 1880-1940', 'Atrocious Misery: The African Origins of Famine in Northern Somalia, 1839-1884', and 'Anglo-Indian Medical Theory and the Origins of Segregation in West Africa'.

The new social history has clearly grown into dominance in Europe and the United States and has become a significant field in India and Japan as well. In 1980, Robert Darnton, who compiled a statistical survey of doctoral dissertations completed in American universities from 1958 to 1968, found that the number of political history studies in 1958 declined to three times more by 1968, and fell below the number of those in social history by 1978. Other traditional history areas such as diplomatic history, intellectual history, and economic history suffered comparable losses and constitutional history had, by 1978, disappeared almost completely as a topic of graduate research.[45] By 1982, Gordon Craig, in his presidential address of the American Historical Association, described the prevailing attitude towards diplomatic and political history as varying 'between condescension and antipathy'.

One American critic of new history has written:

> What is undeniably new (in historical writing) is the triumph of the new (history). In the historical profession as a whole, the new history is now the new orthodoxy. This is not to say that the old history is no longer being written. Political,

> constitutional, diplomatic, military, and intellectual histories continue to be written by some eminent senior historians and even some enterprising young ones. Although more often, the old history is rewritten in light of the new. Thus, political history is quantified and sociologized, and intellectual history... is converted into mentalite history. Yet the old history, if not entirely superseded, has been largely displaced. What was once at the centre of the profession is now at the periphery. What once defined history is now a footnote to history.[46]

The same author, while not condemning new history entirely, nonetheless says of the new trend, "The challenge is serious only because of the dominance (hegemony, the new historian would say) of new history in the profession today."[47] Only a decade ago, it was still possible to speak of the New History. Today, the New History has become so thoroughly familiar, so firmly entrenched in the academy as the old.[48]

Criticism of New History

Despite the new hegemony of new history among the professional ranks in most nations of the world, the trend has not developed totally free from telling criticism. Beyond the allegations of arrogance levelled by Gertrude Himmelfarb and Oscar Handlin, the more serious critiques are directed at the products of new history. One eminent American historian and author of a major book on new history has written that 'often there was impatience with its (new social history) failure to find some underlying pattern, some grand design in the data which it sought to analyse'.[49] British historian Eric Hobsbawm, agreeing with this criticism of new history, has stated in a stronger manner:

> I cannot point to any single work which exemplifies the history of society to which we ought, I believe, to aspire. There have been important advances... toward the study of certain types of society, particularly those based on slavery in North and South

> America or on a large body of peasant cultivators in Europe and Asia. On the other hand, the attempts to translate a comprehensive social history into popular synthesis strike me so far as either relatively unsuccessful or, with all their great merits, not the least of which is stimulation, as schematic and tentative.[50]

Lawrence Stone criticizes what he sees as the deterministic tendency of some of the branches of new history. He has criticized the Marxists for their economic determinism. He reproaches many of the Annalistes for their economic, geographic, and demographic determinism, and he condemns the economic and sociological determinism of the cliometricians. Stone now argues that 'The culture of the group, and even the will of the individual, are potentially at least as important causal agents as the impersonal forces of material output and demographic growth'.[51] Stone speaks for a large majority of the new historians who have an aversion to determinism of all kinds. As Stone has so well stated:

> The basic objection to these threats (assumptions of scientific methodology) to the historical profession is that they all tend to reduce the study of man, and explanation of change, to a simplistic, mechanistic determinism based on some preconceived theoretical notion of universal applicability, regardless of time and space, allegedly verified by scientific laws and scientific methods. Both historians and social scientists must recognize at least three universal constraints on human cognition, which affect all disciplines that are concerned with the nature of man.[52]

Stone, who eloquently reminds us that we should maintain some modesty in our efforts to explore human history, refers us to the sociologist, Robert Nisbet. Nisbet reminds us of three important caveats for any proposed science of man, including history:

> First, awareness of the elements of art that lies in all efforts to grasp reality, no matter how under-girded by pretentious methodologies and computer systems these efforts may be;

> second, however one proceeds, with whatever degree of objectivity and devotion to truth, he cannot escape the limitations imposed by the form of his inquiry; and third, that many worlds through which social scientists, humanists, and others approach reality are unalterably metaphoric.[53]

Another criticism often levelled at new history's analytical style is that its findings are too complex and, therefore, not accessible to the general public. One new historian who seeks a return to a more narrative history writes, "Increasingly, structural, analytical, quantitative historians have found themselves talking to each other and to no one else...." Yet, he finds hope in certain trends in new history: "There is a large audience ready to listen and the new historians are now anxious to speak to that audience, rather than leaving it to be fed on the pabulum of popular biographies and textbooks."[54]

In any return to narrative, the new historians are not likely to go back to political, biographical, or intellectual history as once practised. Though Stone is adamantly opposed to returning to any form of the old history, he does foresee the rise of mentalite history as one route back to narrative without sacrificing the benefits of new history. He proclaims: "This new interest in mental structures has been stimulated by the collapse of traditional intellectual history treated as a kind of paper-chase of ideas back through the ages (which usually ends up with either Aristotle or Plato). 'Great books' were studied in a historical vacuum."[55]

Since new history lacks any general coherence, another crisis results from this confusion – the lack of any consensus on what should be taught in school and university history courses. Existing texts, even those sometimes informed by new history, still cling largely to the old historical narrative and usually concentrate on dynasties or other elites progressing through the ages. Some college courses do require students to read a number of the new history studies. However, students who do often come away with a deep knowledge of witches in a single village, workers in a shoe manufacturing town, or life in a cow town, have gained only a smattering of the historical overview, even of their own nation. As the new historians continue to concentrate on small groups, we will see the gap widening between the ever more esoteric analysis of the new social historians of smaller and smaller units on the one hand, and the students and reading public's lack of accessibility to or interest in this new history on the other.

Still another major criticism of new history is its near-total dependence on social science methods and assumptions. The new history was launched in a sea of social science approaches, yet this relationship has always been uneasy. Some, like Theodore Hammerow, who speaks for those who fear the social science dominance in new history, remind us, "They (the critics of social science techniques) also felt that there is a fundamental difference between history, with its emphases on the individual and the unique, and science, with its quest for the regular and the repetitive."[56] Hammerow cites philosopher Isiah Berlin's warning to historians:

> May it not be that to be unscientific is to defy, for no good logical or empirical reason, established hypotheses and laws, while to be unhistorical is the opposite – to ignore or twist one's view of particular events, persons, predicaments, in the name of laws, theories, principles derived from other fields, logical, ethical, metaphysical, scientific, which the nature of the medium renders inapplicable ... The attempt to construct a discipline which would stand to concrete history as pure to applied, is not a vain hope for something beyond human power, but a chimera, born of a profound incapacity to grasp the nature of natural science, or of history, or of both. What separates the two is not ignorance or prejudice, but a fundamental difference in ultimate purpose.[57]

A further crisis which attends the triumph of new history and which is related to some of the new historians' search for a science of history, is that, as one critic alleges, "in place of the moral imagination, we are more and more confronted with something that might be called the sociological imagination."[58] Himmelfarb goes on to compare many of the new historians to

Mathew Arnold's characterization as barbarians those who were concerned only with the machinery of life. The clear implication of this criticism is that many of the new historians are more interested in patterns, cycles, and structures than in the human story. With the increasing influence of philosophers like Alan Bloom in the United States and the rise of conservative politics around the world (to say nothing of the rising tide of religious fundamentalism), it is clear that some attention is being demanded to the moral dimensions of history by millions of people, even if many of the professional new historians, except some Marxist historians, are indifferent to this demand.

Conclusion

It seems apparent that the techniques, methods, subjects, and assumptions of new history are here for the foreseeable future, even as the critics have all but rejected the early promise of both cliometrics and psychohistory. With the new dominance of anthropology in history writing, narrative possibilities, as Stone suggests, are abundant. This trend could mean a new accessibility to the wider public. However, the major problem raised by Hobsbawm, the lack of synthesis in the new history, still remains. Despite some remarkable studies of small towns, and of long neglected social groups such as slaves, workers, women, and peasants, there has been no real attempt at integrating these studies with what was previously known or even with each other. The new history is still a potpourri of brilliant individual studies without a larger integration or coherence. This growing collection of small-scale studies has not added up to a general history of anything.

New history is no longer really new. Rather, as one of its well-known practitioners says, "The past twenty-five years will come to be seen as something of a heroic phase in the evolution of historical understanding, squeezed in between two periods of quiet consolidation of received wisdom."[59] Another member of the new history school now says:

> Indeed, the new history as a whole can now be seen as less radical or innovative than it had first appeared. .... It seemed to offer a way out of the obsolescence with which the discipline was threatened. ...It held out the promise of revitalized scholarship relevant to the needs of a changing society...it was a time of ferment and rejuvenation, of pioneering and iconoclasticism. But that period is now drawing to a close, and we can see it more clearly than in its intoxicating springtime.[60]

If the new history is now at least middle aged and the profession may be ready for a 'new' new history, it is still apparent that the achievements of new history have been considerable. From a history of elites in politics, administration and diplomacy and war, new history has moved our attention to ordinary people, both men and women and to their everyday concerns and meanings of life. Out of this new mass history, people in the so-called Third World have entered into the historical consciousness of Western history for the first time, and billions of new subjects have become part of our historical consciousness. These achievements alone add up to a significant accomplishment in the field of history.

Perhaps, at this juncture of uncertainty in history, when retrenchment in the field is a trend everywhere, it is time to begin the integration of new history with the old. New history has found studies of elites of any kind an anathema, yet in our daily lives, we know that people around us who possess great power, wealth, and influence do indeed affect our lives.

As one historian points out, if the people of power are of no account in history, how is it that we look first to find what they are doing, in our daily papers. At some point, new history will have to go beyond its bias against the rich and powerful since their acts make an impact on us.

Retaining openness has always characterized history as a field. One of the leaders of the history profession has warned: ".... If the profession does indeed begin to narrow its viewpoint and closes off its intellectual options, as it certainly did in the early 20th century, it runs the risk either of growing sterility or of factional fragmentation."[61] In vociferously holding out for openness, the writer warns that 'only if the two principles of methodological diversity and ideological pluralism are vigorously defended will the necessary intellectual interchange between the historian and the social scientist continue to be a fruitful one'.[62]

History has a long history. It has experienced a lot of 'new histories'. What has happened and what will continue to happen is for historians and history to be judged not so much on its interests and focus, but on its attention to sources and criticism, its style of writing, in sum its quality as scholarship. Talented historians can make sense and communicate meaning from the most unconventional sources. Histories from all ages are still read with fascination.

New history must now begin to take its place in that long tradition of historical interpretation and writing.

Notes

1. Herbert Butterfield, *The Whig Interpretation of History*, Oxford, London, 1931.
2. Lawrence Stone, *Past and Present*, Routledge and Kegan Paul, London, 1981, p. 7.
3. When the *Annales*, as it became popularly known, moved from Strasbourg to Paris, one of its editors, Marc Bloch, took a position at the Sorbonne and the other editor, Lucien Febvre, joined the College de France. After World War II, the Ecole Pratique des Hautes Etudes established the Sixime Section, and the Annalistes then rested on a firm institutional base. Under its editors, Lucien Febvre and Marc Bloch, the journal and the school survived the depression and the German occupation, and after World War II, under the editorship of Fernand Braudel, the journal grew to become one of the most important influences in the entire world of history.
4. Marc Bloch, *Strange Defeat: A Statement of Evidence Written in 1940*, (tr.) Gerard Hopkins, New York, 1968, pp. 172-73.
5. Fernand Braudel, *The Mediterranean and the Mediterranean World in the Age of Philip II*, (tr.) Sian Reynolds, Harper and Row, New York, 1972, Vol. I, p. 21.

6. Ironically, many others at the time of this writing, saw the chaos of Europe as resulting from the charismatic force of a single man and from an ideology that had mobilized the German people.
7. Fernand Braudel, 'Personal Testimony', *Journal of Modern History*, December 1982, p. 454.
8. Braudel, *The Mediterranean...*, Vol. II, p. 1244.
9. Jacques Le Goff, 'Is Politics Still the Backbone of History?' *Daedalus*, 100, 1971, pp. 4, 12.
10. This three-tiered paradigm owed much to Marxist ideas of base and superstructure. It also shares with Marxism a materialist conception for belief in historical determinism.
11. Emmanuel Le Roy-Ladurie, *The Territory of the Historian*, University of Chicago Press, Chicago, p. 111.
12. Emmanuel Le Roy-Ladurie, 'L'histoire immobile', in *The Territory of the Historian*, Quoted in Stone, op. cit., p. 79.
13. Emmanuel Le Roy-Ladurie, op. cit., p. 285.
14. The term, 'new social history', can be a deceiving term. Within the movement, there have been and continue to be vicious arguments over what is worth doing and how it should be done best. Meanwhile, the more traditional historians such as Oscar Handlin, Gertrude Himmelfarb and J.H. Hexter have continued to attack the new social historians both for their interpretations and for their arrogance.
15. Stone, op. cit., p. 13.
16. Robert Kelly, 'Culture as History', *The New York Times*, July 19, 1978, (opposite Editorial page).
17. Peter Berger and Thomas Luckman, *The Social Construction of Reality*, Anchor Books, New York, 1967, p. 18.
18. Quoted in Stone, op. cit., p. 16.
19. Stephen Thernstrom, *The Other Bostonians*, Harvard University Press, Cambridge, 1973.
20. Paul Johnson, *The Shopkeepers' Millennium Society and Revival in Rochester New York*, Hill and Wang, New York, 1978.
21. Harold Dyos and Michael Wolff (eds.), *The Victorian City: Images and Realities*, Routledge & Kegan Paul, London, 1973.
22. Examples of family studies include Gutman, Herbert, *The Black Family in Slavery and Freedom*, Pantheon Books, New York, 1976; Philip Aries, *Centuries of Childhood*, Basic Books, New York, 1965; David Hunt, *Parents and Children in History, The Psychology of Family Life in Early Modern France*, Basic Books, New York, 1970.

23. Quoted in Stone, op. cit., pp. 36, 37.
24. Emmanuel Le Roy-Ladurie, *Montaillou,* Vintage Books, New York, 1979.
25. Emmanuel Le Roy-Ladurie, *The Territory of the Historian*, p. 223.
26. Lawrence Stone, 'Revival of Narrative', *Daedalus*, 100, 1971, p. 21.
27. E.J. Hobsbawm, 'From Social History to the History of Society', *Daedalus*, 100, 1971, p. 33.
28. So too had immigration historians' works, such as Marcus Lee Hansen's *The Atlantic Migration,* and political historians works, such as Crane Brinton's *The Jacobins,* tried to use statistics in their 1930s books.
29. David Herlihy, 'Quantification in the 1980s: Numerical and Formal Analysis in European History', *Journal of Interdisciplinary Studies*, 12, (1981-82), p. 135.
30. Robert W. Fogel and Stanley L. Engerman, *Time of the Cross: The Economics of American Negro Slavery*, Boston, Little Brown, 1974.
31. Oscar Handlin, *Truth in History,* Harvard University Press, Cambridge, 1979, pp. 11.
32. David Landes, 'On Avoiding Babel', *Journal of Economic History,* 38 1978, pp. 6-10.
33. Harry Elmer Barnes, 'Psychology and History: Some Reasons for Predicting Their More Active Cooperation in the Future', *American Journal of Psychology*, 30, 1919, pp. 362.
34. H. Stuart Hughes, *History as Art and as Science: Twin Vistas on the Past,* University of Chicago Press, Chicago, 1964.
35. Phillipe Aries, *Centuries of Childhood*, Knopf, New York, 1962.
36. Stanley Elkins, *Slavery: A Problem in American Institutional and Intellectual Life*, University of Chicago Press, Chicago, 1968.
37. Bruce Mazlish, *In Search of Nixon: A Psychological Inquiry*, Basic Books, New York, 1972, p. 154.
38. Handlin, *Truth in History*, pp. 273-74.
39. Stone, op. cit., p. 9.
40. Carl Schorske, 'Politics and the Psyche in *Fin de Siecle* Vienna: Schnitzler and Hofmannsthal', *American Historical Review*, 66, No. 4. July 1961, pp. 930-46; 'Politics in a New Key: An Austrian Triptych' *Journal of Modern History*, 39, No. 4, December 1967.
41. See Lawrence Stone, 'Prosopography', *Daedelus*, Winter 1971.

42. Robert Darnton, 'Intellectual and Cultural History', Michael Kammen (ed.), *The Past Before Us: Contemporary Historical Writing in the United States*, Cornell University Press, Ithaca, N.Y., pp. 350-51.
43. Emmanuel Le Roy-Ladurie, *Territory of the Historian*, p. 111.
44. Ibid.
45. Robert Darnton, op. cit., p. 353.
46. Gertrude Himmelfarb, *The New History and the Old*, The Harvard University Press, Cambridge, 1987, p. 4.
47. Ibid. p. 5.
48. Gertrude Himmelfarb, 'Review of the Past and the Present', in *New York Times Book Review*, January 1982, p. 9.
49. Hammerow, *Reflections on History and Historians*, University of Wisconsin Press, Madison, Wisconsin, 1987, p. 186.
50. E.H. Hobsbawm, 'Social History to History of Society', *Daedalus*, 100, 1971, pp. 42-43.
51. Lawrence Stone, *Past and Present*, Routledge and Kegan Paul, London, 1981, pp. xi-xii.
52. Ibid, p. 42.
53. Ibid, p. 42.
54. Ibid, p. 87.
55. Ibid, p. 86.
56. Hammerow, op. cit., p. 185.
57. Isiah Berlin, 'History and Theory: The Concept of Scientific History', Astrid Bernz (ed.), *History and Theory: Studies in the Philosophy of History*, Wesleyan University Press, Middletown, 1972, 1, p. 31.
58. Himmelfarb, op. cit., p. 49.
59. Stone, op. cit., xi.
60. Hammerow, op. cit., p. 198.
61. Lawrence Stone, op. cit., p. 43.
62. Lawrence Stone, 'History and the Social Sciences', in *Past and Present*, p. 44.

2

Relevance of Recording the Past

Aniket Jaaware

Let me begin with some elementary observations, some of them rather obvious, some crude, and some possibly obscure. The first is that a historian writes about past things and persons and relations between things and persons, and persons and persons, but her own writing is invariably concerned with her own social, cultural, political, and academic conditions. She can only bring to her work concepts and categories that are available, or that which she can think up. The second is that in as much as she writes about the past, she must have some notion of how the past, the present, and the future relate to each other she must also think about what her understanding is of these relations between the three kinds of time. In short, she must, consciously or unconsciously, possess a certain notion of time. This may or may not be reflected in her writing, as a historian, but she must have a certain concept, a certain understanding.

It is always possible for a historian to talk about the past without any of the above, in what we might call a naive historical manner, the way we as non-historians talk about the past, freely, without worrying about method, or concepts of time. There are historians who write about the past as if it was something gone away forever, as if it never makes the present different. The past is reduced to dates, figures, and genealogies, names of kings and queens, or nationalist leaders. School textbook history often tends to be like this, the students never get to know and understand why all these things are important, so they mug up dates and names, and manage to pass in the examination. This is what we could designate as the simple past: something dead and gone, but remembered for some other strictly non-historical purpose. We could say this is one type of naive historiography. There is yet another naive historiography, which *forgets* the fact that the past is dead and gone. This kind of historiography forgets the present, and seeks to bring alive the past. A lot of Marathi historiography around Shivaji is of this kind. It makes the past present to us in charming and emotionally powerful ways. Such history is very close to drama or film. It is not surprising that the lines get blurred, and that historians can write plays, and novelists can write historical novels, and be given some authority in history writing as well. This variety of history writing is as harmful as the school textbook variety. Both these are harmful, I am suggesting, because they do not address the question of how all these relate to us as living and changing human beings, living in a society of other living and changing human beings.

I have said these are two naive forms of historiography. What is naive about them is that they do not possess, or care to possess, any notion of time and the relations between the past, the present, and the future. The first variety of naïve historiography presumes, without examination, that the past is past, *dead and gone*, and therefore meaningless; the other variety of naïve historiography presumes that the past is *the present* and therefore more meaningful than the present, and thus attempts to re-enact the past in the present, which is wrong, because the past and the present are two different moments in time, as all of us know intuitively. As I tried to point out in the beginning, our understanding of time is very crucial for our view of history as such.

There cannot be much doubt that the past goes away, but what is interesting in history is at which present moment, and in which aspect of the present moment which part of the past is brought back, at which moment we recall items from the past. Consider how, for several years, *The Times of India*, and other newspapers used to print Gandhi's picture on the front page every October 2nd. *The Times* stopped doing it a few years ago, as did most newspapers. This is a crucial moment in the history of the media, and their relationship with nationalism. *The Hindu*, on the other hand, did a major photo-series this year on Gandhi. The implications for memory are clear, I think. We recall only those things that we need. It is the task of the historian to remind us of things that we do not normally recall. Please remember that there is a difference between memory and recall. Recall is voluntary, remembering something can be involuntary. I will come back to this issue of memory later.

Immediately, an objection can be raised. It can be said, for example, that history in fact has nothing to do with memory because history is concerned with facts and records; history, as Aristotle used to say, has to do with what happened. There is a whole mechanism, perhaps even a method to history, a method of establishing authenticity of documents, of items, and this method is far more empirical than, for example, the methods available in literary analysis. This view of history tells us that we cannot make a statement about the past without any solid empirical, preferably documentary, evidence. Thus, the picture of the historian emerges: totally engrossed in the past, pottering about in dusty archives, among ancient crumbling papers, totally unaware of what is happening around her, unaware of the present. Let us consider this in more detail.

If I want to know what year Shakespeare was born, how do I find out? It is very easy, for a biography of Shakespeare will tell us that. But suppose we are interested in verifying the date, how will we do it? How did the Schoenbaum, one of Shakespeare's biographers, find out? We can only suppose that he got it from other books. Then we are forced to ask, how did the first historian verify the date of Shakespeare's birth?

Well, we are talking of times far back from us, and we must assume that there were no municipalities requiring that births be registered. That kind of documentation was not required in those days. However, the church did keep a record of births and deaths, written down in books. So what we have to do then is go to Stratford-upon-Avon, go to the church there, and ask for their birth listings. All this while, we are hoping that these have survived, and we have not yet wondered whether the church that we visit today is the same church that existed when baby William was born. We will keep these doubts aside for a moment. Let us say, the church has the record, so we look up the lists, and find an entry there, saying William Shakespeare, son of John Shakespeare, and let us say there is a date after the name. We can now say that we have authenticated the birth date for the good Bill Shakespeare. But wait, there is a slight problem. How do we trust the record? Let us imagine the situation: There is Shakespeare's mother, who cannot go to the church and say that she has just had a baby. The father might go. But was it necessary in those days to immediately record a birth or a death? No, it wasn't because that kind of record keeping was not required. We know from other instances that the church kept a record of the date of baptism, rather than the date of birth. So the date we have could very well be when the little baby, crying, without doubt, was sprinkled with holy water and the name of William given to it, in the presence of the priest, the godfather and godmother, and the parents. The date could very well be that of the baptism, not of the birth.

Let me give another instance. We have the date for the first printing of a book – it is, say, July 24, 1564. We are proud of this knowledge, but a little investigation reveals that this is *not* the date for the printing of the Gutenberg *Bible*, but the binding of the printed pages into a book. The printing itself could very well have been completed two or three days before.

The point I am trying to make is that verification of such simple things like dates requires extra knowledge of social practices. We must know that it was customary to put the date of binding as the date of printing, and that churches often recorded the date of baptism, rather than of the birth itself. Where are we going to get this knowledge from? From other history books, obviously. So what we have here is an example of some books of history being used to authenticate some other books of history. We are lost in a world of documents, from which any empirical fact refuses to emerge!

It would seem that this is the view of history that most people take – of history as issues mostly irrelevant, and of historians lost in documents that nobody reads. Needless to say, this is not an interesting view of history at all, because history affects us in very many profound, and often violent and disturbing, ways. I will come to this point again.

Possibly the most interesting view of history emerges in the period that we know as the Romantic period. Naturally, I am talking of Europe in general, but Germany in particular. We are talking of a period that is known as the period that immediately followed the French Revolution, the so-called Enlightenment period. I am using the conventional periodization for the sake of convenience and easy communicability. It is in this period immediately following the Enlightenment, it is with the dominance and popularity of G.W.F. Hegel, and his description of the dialectic that the word 'history' now acquires a completely different meaning – as a temporal process of the unfolding of the dialectic, moving in a spiral towards ever higher, ever more absolute knowledge. Please note that this is the philosophical base for the dominant view of history. Historians themselves do not have to be aware of this. Therefore, I can avoid explaining in greater detail what the philosophical notion of the Hegelian dialectic is. It should also be noted that this dialectical notion of history is quite different from the simpler cause and effect model of history. The simpler cause and effect model of history can be very easily parodied: For example, I could say that I am here in this world, such as I am, because my great-great-grandfather was very wealthy. Because he was wealthy, he could travel a lot, because he travelled a lot, he met a beautiful woman not of his caste or area, fell in love with her and, despite odds, married her. If that marriage had not taken place, I would not be in this world, would I? I think the dialectical model of history is far more difficult to parody, and especially so because the Hegelian dialectic is more complex than our understanding of the concepts of cause and effect.

Basically, we would have to wait till the Annales School to move away from the dialectical model of history. In that sense, the Annales School histories already show a fundamental structuralist impulse: The idea is, if we take large chunks of time and write histories – these will essentially be 'synchronic' histories – then 'patterns' emerge, which we would not be able to see otherwise. Another typical gesture of the Annales School is to take a place, and write a history of it across a very large chunk of time, as evident in Le Roy-Ladurie's history of the place called Montaillou. In a wonderful book called *Jasmin's Witch*, Le Roy-Ladurie shows how a minor literary text can produce a most interesting history around it, and through it. I suppose the best example for what I am paradoxically calling synchronic history is Fernand Braudel's three volumes, *Capitalism and Civilization*.

It is a common place assertion, in historiography, that the aspect of history that a historian concerns herself with is determined by her present concerns. This is best exemplified, I think, in the number of biographical-historical accounts of Shivaji that have come up in the last thirty years on the one hand, and the increase in our historical knowledge of women in India and in other cultures as well on the other hand. This allows us to bring out the somewhat neglected aspect of history, that is the written histories: that history is a matter of social, public memory. When a society, or a social group, begins to think of itself as war-like, that is to say, aggressive perhaps out of necessity (one can always pass off one's choice as necessity), it is to be expected that this social group will remember, and will want to remember positively, some of its war-like heroes. Nationalism in the present makes all our historical warriors look contemporary nationalists. Our interest in feminism makes the lives of all women in history interesting in themselves. I do not mean to suggest that this is a bad thing, but it can become bad if we forget that historical figures are figures from the past, dead and gone. In short, an interest in history which disallows us to see the difference between the past and the present can become harmful. Allow me to give another example: It is, very crudely speaking, because we do not have progress in the Western sense of the world, it is because we do not have the kinds of missiles that the US or the UK has, that we feel the need to assert that in the past, we had them before the West. Please note that it is present psychology, or mentality, which is making us look for aeroplanes and atomic power in the *Vedas*. Such histories tell us more about our present than our past, I think. They tell us what we think we lack right now, at the present time. Therefore, strictly speaking, these books are about the present, not about the past at all.

I would like to point out that there is, after all, a dialectic operating here in such histories – a dialectic between the perception of a present lack, and the desire to think well of ourselves, as strong and so on, which is imaginatively filled in by a strange historiography. The work of the negative is rather obvious in these processes. In that sense, such histories that find evidence of glory or technology in the past are entirely within the Western tradition. Let us not forget, for example, how the West created its own origin in the Greek civilization before and during the Renaissance, more particularly, and in a more developed form in the 18th and 19th centuries. Aristotle's texts, especially *Poetics,* for example, was not available to mediaeval Europe – it became available only around the 14th century through Arabic sources – commentaries, translations, and so on. Martin Bernal has written a rather thick book, called *The Black Athena*, which shows how the West does not acknowledge the origins of Greek civilization in ancient Egypt.

After these preliminaries, allow me to get a little more technical. I have already asserted that what we understand by the word history and what we understand of our past, as individuals and as societies, depends on our understanding of time as individuals and as societies. Our understanding of time will depend on a variety of things - our religion, our philosophy, and our sciences. I will not attempt a detailed comparison of different notions of time here. But allow me to give a brief description, restricting myself to unexamined descriptions, which almost amount to clichés.

If we can go by Aristotle at all, the understanding of time in the Greek civilization was more interested in its calculability. Time, as Aristotle pointed out in his *Physics,* is calculable by motion, where motion is defined as change of place. The Christian notion of time, on the other hand, was not so much interested in the calculability of time as in events that take place in time - the creation of time by God, as he created the sun and the moon, and then the painful, impatient, fearful and rather long wait for the Day of Judgement are the two terminal points in time. Time, in fact, now has a beginning and an ending. Time is now linear. This linearity is different from the linearity of time as Aristotle described it - time as a series of 'now-points' that come from the future and recede into the past. To put it quickly, Christian time had a goal to reach, it had a teleology - the Judgement Day. There were some very early Christian sects which had worked out the geography and chronology of the Second Coming so well that members of this sect used to go to a specific place and wait for Christ to come again a second time. As Walter Benjamin said once, "I think the notion of time in Judaism can be pictured like an open door through which the Messiah can walk in any time, any moment."

I will not be able to talk about the Hindu notion of time because I do not know much about it, but I am told it is a cyclical notion of time. It is not unexpected then that history might repeat itself, presumably as a farce. Neither would I be able to say anything about the notion of time in Islam, but I imagine there must be some similarities between monotheistic religions and their conceptions of time.

Naturally, when we talk of history in the modern times, which is to say after the 19th century, we are talking about secular time, by which I mean non-religious time. This conception of time is firmly dominated by the natural sciences. This time is not marked by social or communal – in the good sense – meaning at all. This time is marked by its infinite divisibility, by its minute calculability, and thus is quite separated from the kind of meaningful time that we experience as persons or as members of some social group. Jacques Le Goff, in his very well-known essay, 'Merchant's Time and Church's Time in the Middle Ages',[1] demonstrates how notions of time affect culture and, in return, culture affects notions of time. He also mentions how, in 1355, an official authorized the construction of a bell-tower in the town of Aire-sur-la-Lys. What is interesting about this bell-tower and the ringing of bells on the tower is that these are *not* rung for any religious purpose, but for marking the time for textile workers to begin and to stop working. Historically speaking, I could say that Taylorism began as far back in time as 1355, for the management of work according to some notion of time management, and not human wish or desire or need, seems to be working here already. This is something of an exaggeration, obviously. But there does seem to be a pattern in the way the relationship between labour and time changed in the West. Perhaps we could call this pattern capitalism. I do not know.

As I tried to say in the beginning, our understanding of the difference between religious, or sacred, time and non-religious, or profane, time is very important for our understanding of history and of the past, Let me not belabour the point, and move on to the next one, which is equally important.

As we all know, history must be written in some language. This is a strictly historical matter because history changed fundamentally after the invention of photography, and after the invention of motion picture photography, and then after the invention of the live telecast. Histories written in this century perhaps will not be only in language, but in the visual media. This is already happening, as we know in the television reportage on the Gulf, the Afghan, and the Iraq assaults. I will not talk here of the visual media for the simple reason that the business of television is to manufacture the present, and at this moment, I am more interested in history, which has to do with the past and with what happened, and not in live telecasts, not with what is supposed to be happening right in front of my eyes.

The fact that histories are mostly written in language must be taken to imply that histories will have all the strengths and weaknesses that language has. If a table is made out of wood, it will burn, however ugly or beautiful, shallow or profound, useful or useless it may be. Histories are susceptible to all the diseases that language is capable of contracting, or generating by itself. Histories can have auto-immune-disorder syndromes, if language is capable of such a syndrome. I think in the 20th century, we owe, as historians, a little to Hayden White, who wrote a book called *Tropics of Discourse.* Or perhaps to Derrida, who wrote an essay titled 'White Mythologies: Metaphor in the Text of Philosophy'.

History tells us a story of the past, as does historical fiction. History tells a story, as does fiction. History selects certain facts from a plethora of facts, and sets these facts in a certain order, chronological, causal, and historical. Now, the most interesting thing is that this is precisely what a storyteller, a novelist, does, is it not? She selects, and combines certain fictitious facts so as to construct a story. Consider a sentence like "Five years passed". One can come across such a sentence in history as much as in a novel or a short story. It is obvious that the author thinks that the events that took place in that time are of no significance. Consider how, for a long time, Western historians jumped from the first century of Christianity into the Renaissance, glossing over a large chunk of time, calling it 'the Dark Ages'. Consider how our own histories tend to neglect the so-called mediaeval period. We have less knowledge of the food habits and dress habits of that period. I am not sure we have documented evidence for what the soldiers ate when they followed Shivaji on his road to Surat.

It is now reasonably well known in linguistics and language studies that the languages used in literature and other kinds of writing are not very different from each other. The essay by Derrida that I mentioned before shows this in philosophically interesting ways. If further evidence is needed, one can consider a scientist's writings on science and language: Werner Heisenberg's essay on the language of science, for example. This allows us to say that written or spoken histories are as linguistic and textual as literature is, and have more to do with language than with past facts. This is an exaggeration, of course, but there is a point to this. For centuries, philosophers and historians have written their works, and ignored the medium in which they were writing them. For a historian, the language she uses is merely a vehicle that takes her readers to post facts, other documents, to certain intellectual hypotheses about what cause led to what effect, and so on. But as we know, language imposes its own imperatives, strengths, and defects on everything we say and write, including the most personal things. I see no reason why philosophy or history should be spared the decay built into language as such. Please do not be misled by my imagery of decay and disease – language can do some very nice things, too, but I wonder if historians are interested in these nice things. All this is only to remind ourselves that historians are susceptible to diseases of language and may not be able to reach those healthy empirical facts of the past. The same is true for other disciplines, including philosophy.

Thus, we come to the realization that history is a narrative. There is already in place a reasonable description of narrative in literary studies, and historians and theoreticians of history began to realize that this description, and the analytical method that follows from it, could be used to analyse historical narratives as well. Concepts from literary criticism of the novel and the narrative in general could now be used to understand historical narratives. This is partly seen in Ranajit Guha's use of concepts from Barthes' 'Introduction to the Structural Analysis of Narrative' in his *Elementary Aspects of Peasant Revolt.* It would not be an exaggeration that the extraordinary changes that took place in literary theory in the 1970s and 1980s filtered into other disciplines, most significantly into philosophy and history. It seemed, in those days, that everything was a narrative, everything had a literary character to it, including history and philosophy. Having found narrative, we looked for it everywhere.

Thus, historiography came to a self-realization – that historians systematically set up a story, consciously and unconsciously, and it became one of the critical tasks of historiography to be alert to what was not included in the story, what was consciously and, even more interestingly, unconsciously excluded from the narrative structure. Please note that this is not a matter of failing to use some available resource or getting a fact wrong. These mistakes are easily made and equally easily corrected. But in the very setting up of the story, in the very 'emplotment', as we used to say, there are certain exclusions, omissions, and so on. These we used to call the 'silences' in the text.

From a different trajectory, using ideas from psychoanalysis, Althusser and Pierre Macherey came up with the notion of a 'symptomatic reading' – a reading which treats these 'silences' as symptoms in the manner of psychoanalysis, but undertakes a more or less Marxian interpretation of these symptoms.

It was around this time that Michel Foucault published his study of madness in the past, under the general title of *History of Madness.* A social thinker, Foucault also had a philosophical investment in the project, an investment that takes a trajectory very different from Habermas and his notion of emancipation. This involved a much stronger critique of what we call the Enlightenment Rationality. This was not just a matter of stating or proving that the Enlightenment ideas were merely bourgeois or inconsistent. It was a question of how these ideas were deployed to bring about a society that could be measured and calculated in specific ways. Foucault's *Discipline and Punish: The Birth of the Prison* systematically demonstrates, through a historical analysis of modes of punishment, how society changed and how society remained the same in some other ways. The popular notion that Foucault is a 'philosopher of ruptures' is somewhat misleading. There are interviews and articles in which he clearly states that he takes this to be an exaggerated representation of his work. I will talk about this later, if required.

Foucault's treatment of historical problems, informed with a new method of thinking about things, has naturally seen extremely influential European intellectual activity in several fields. Neither can we ignore it, since it is, after all, an innovative way of thinking about the past and its relationship with us. Several historians have objections to Foucault's work from a historical point of view, and the debate between Marcel Leonard and Foucault is perhaps instructive. This is to be found again in the second volume of *French Studies in History,* an Indian publication, and available in a completely inexpensive form.

Finally, we may now come to the work presented over nine volumes by Subaltern Studies Collective. Taking ideas from Antonio Gramsci and modifying them a little, I believe, to suit the context in which they were writing, the Collective has effected a fundamental change in our attitude to the official history of the so-called national freedom struggle, and in our attitude to the 19th century. Needless to say, the work presented in these volumes is varied, and sometimes disparate. The Collective has also given us a way of reading documents generated in the colonial period in such a way as to give us some picture of the subaltern person, the subaltern group. It is well known that in the initial stages, there was a tendency in the Collective to attempt to bring to life the subaltern consciousness itself, as it were, before the readers. In two or three of her essays, Spivak points out the intellectual and ethical risks in this attempt, the better known of these is her essay, 'Can the Subaltern Speak?'

Having given a hasty review of some of the major tendencies in historiography, it is perhaps now time to ask, what then is history for us ? What do we mean when we say 'we'? Allow me to speculate a little, after which I shall bring this speech to its close.

In these troublous times, in which one may confuse between god, epic character, and historical figure, history becomes particularly relevant, but it all depends on what is meant by history all over again. Is it not remarkable that the kind of historians who claim that there was this or that technology present in the ancient glorious Hindu past feel the need to *prove* these statements by offering *evidence*? However cooked up the history might be, I find it really remarkable that they feel this need. While claiming to be anti-colonial, such histories are firmly within the colonial tradition of historiography where one could say anything without 'evidence'. I suggest that this category of evidence needs to be examined yet again. We need not be naively empiricist and insist on documentary evidence, we may allow ourselves a little speculation here and there, and we may want to formulate a way of relating to history that allows us a freer notion of evidence. Let me allude to the Annales School notion of mentality, the attempt at a history of mentality. This was a fine idea, I think, because this is one aspect of our human life that is the least susceptible to documentation. The lover speaking tenderly to the beloved, the child crying for food, these leave precious few records, and thus there is the greatest tension between psychology and history, but quite obviously, the emotional life of the people is probably what is, at present, of much importance to them. So, historians must find a way of writing a history of emotions. Lucien Febvre's essay on this subject, in the first volume of *French Studies in History*, is instructive in this respect.

I will not address the well-known issue of history in India. I mean the apparent lack of historical records, because it is quite obvious that what constitutes a historical record, what constitutes evidence, would change as our notion of human life, our notion of history, changes. There is some truth in what Hegel says somewhere, I believe, that India has no history. Let us not immediately raise our anti-colonial hackles and start grimacing. I imagine this is not something terribly bad, for Hegel was talking in terms of prevalent Western tradition. As is well known again, in the Romantic period, all manner of things were said about India and the Orient in general, which were not really about India or the Orient because these were mere excuses for instituting the romantic criticism of European society. The comment actually is about European philosophy. Just as some of our historical books are more about the present than about the past, all these romantic accounts of India and the Orient are about Europe, and not about what their explicit subject matter is. There is a play of desire here, and we must be sensitive to it.

Finally, let me come to the issue of how the past comes back to us, and how social memory operates in this coming back. It is clear already that we believe we are free of the colonial period, and are trying hard to forget it. We remember the atrocities of the Mughal period far more easily nowadays than the atrocities in the British period. When I say we, I am talking about public and social memory, dominated by Hindu sentiment. This is where historians have to come in, and correct public and social memory. This deflection of memory from the immediate past to the distant past is curious, I think, and needs to be understood. No doubt, some present necessities are forcing us to neglect, or willfully forget, the British period nowadays. It seems to me that our present interest in collaborating with Western industries and promise of economic growth makes it necessary for us that we, as a Hindu community, do not want to share our profits with others and, moreover, we cannot afford to offend these agencies of so-called growth any more, and this makes us look for other enemies.

There are a lot of things that could still be said, but I am after all not a historian. I have no training in historical methodology and, though I like reading histories, I cannot bring to the subject the specific expertise of the specialist. I hope you will be patient with what I have said here and now.

Note

1. "Merchant's Time and Church's Time in the Middle Ages', in *French Studies in History*, Vol. II, *The Departures,* Maurice Aymard and Harbans Mukhia (ed.), New Delhi, Orient Longman, 1990, pp. 103-213.

3

Orientalism and History

Raja Dixit

Orientalism is a very broad and equally complex theme. It is a cultural and political phenomenon. Orientalism, at once, can be understood as (1) Oriental studies/scholarship, (2) a mode of discourse, and (3) an instrument of hegemony. The word 'Orientalist' also implies different shades of meaning. In the Indian context, 18th and 19th century scholars such as William Jones,[1] Charles Wilkins,[2] Henry Colebrooke,[3] and F. Max Muller,[4] who conducted the Oriental/Indological studies, are generally termed as the Orientalists. Their curiosity about the Orient, coupled with British administrative needs, led to their research pursuits. It laid down the foundation of Orientalist scholarship, of which Indology was an offshoot.

In the initial stage of British colonialism in India, there were a number of ideological currents pertaining to the administration and education in India. Among them was the above-mentioned school of Orientalists, which showed respect for the Indian cultural tradition. It was also in favour of imparting education through the vernacular medium in India. The views of these Orientalists resembled those of conservatives like Edmund Burke. They were against imposing sudden changes on Indian society and indiscriminately uprooting indigenous ideas and institutions. Rather, they advocated the gradualist approach and aimed at combining the indigenous and English ideas and institutions. Some British administrators in India such as Thomas Munro, Mount Stuart Elphinstone, and Charles Metcalfe also held identical views. The early Orientalists were influenced by the contemporary Romanticist trend in some respects. The Anglicist School opposed the views of this group. They included thinkers and administrators such as James Mill, Lord William Bentinck, and Lord Macaulay. They regarded India and Indian culture as inferior to that of the West. The early Orientalists believed that the Indian tradition was originally very rich, but that it had deteriorated in the course of time. The Anglicists, on the contrary, believed that the Indian tradition was weak and inferior right from the beginning. They emphasized the 'intrinsic inferiority' of the Orient/India. They aimed at modernizing India by popularizing modern science and learning through education. They wanted to impose Western values, principles, and institutions on India and thereby anglicize India. These views were best reflected in James Mill's *History of British India* (1818) and Macaulay's *Despatch on Education* (1835). On February 2, 1835, Macaulay proclaimed: "We must at present do our best to form a class who may be interpreters between us and the millions whom we govern – a class of persons Indian in blood and colour, but English in tastes, in opinions, in morals, and in intellect." The Anglicist intellectuals and administrators were greatly influenced by 'liberalism' and 'utilitarianism'.[5] The third school is known as the 'evangelical' school, composed mainly of Christian missionaries. In England, the evangelicals differed sharply from the liberal and utilitarian thinkers. But in India, the proselytizing spirit, civilizing mission, and commercial interests of these two groups combined under the cover of British imperialism. Evangelicals such as Charles Grant, William Wilberforce, and Alexander Duff made Indian culture and religions (especially Hinduism and Islam) the targets of their criticism. In this respect, they matched with the

Anglicists. In fact, the evangelicals' views on India were basically Anglicist.

The Orientalists could be thus classified into two broad categories: (1) the early Orientalist scholars, and (2) the Anglicists (liberals-utilitarians and evangelicals). The views of these groups on the Orient and on India were not identical. But both the groups basically represented Western imperialism. They looked towards the Orient through the lens of Western superiority. Edward Said[6] includes along with these two groups even G.W.F. Hegel and Karl Marx in the tradition of Orientalists. Both Hegel and Marx emphasized the stagnant nature of Indian society. Said includes among the Orientalists a very large mass of writers, among whom are poets, novelists, philosophers, political theorists, economists, and imperial administrators. Said highlighted the alliance between Orientalism and imperialism. It was due to Said's book, *Orientalism*, (1978) that the terms, Orientalism and Orientalists, acquired a specific meaning. As Albert Hourani wrote to Edward Said in March 1992, due to the force of his argument, Said's book had the 'unfortunate effect' of making it almost impossible to use the term Orientalism in a neutral sense, so much had it become a term of abuse.[7] The indigenous Orientalist scholarship in India is sometimes referred to as 'in-house Orientalism'.

In a critical discussion of Orientalism, Said's book could be regarded as a landmark. Due to the vast scope of the theme, Said stated that it seemed to him foolish to attempt an encyclopaedic narrative history of Orientalism. Therefore, he concentrated mainly on Europe's experience of the Near Orient, or of Islam, and referred to Europe's experience of the Far Orient wherever necessary. He limited his set of questions to the Anglo-French-American experience of the Arabs and Islam, which, for almost a thousand years, together stood for the Orient.[8] His views and findings, however, are generally applicable to the remaining parts of the Orient, including India.

Said's analysis of Orientalism is based mainly on the following four concepts: (1) knowledge-power relationship,

(2) East-West binary opposition, (3) Michel Foucault's concept of discourse, and (4) Antonio Gramsci's concept of hegemony. In this regard, Kate Currie says, "While the Foucauldian notion of discourse has enabled Said to identify Orientalism, it is the Gramscian notion of cultural hegemony operating within civil society that gives Orientalism its durability. The influence of the Italian Marxist Gramsci on Said is as powerful as that of Foucault. Indeed, Said's search for a 'critical consciousness' – 'a space between the dominant culture and totalizing forms of a critical system – owes more to Gramsci than Foucault."[9]

"The Orient," says Edward Said, "was almost a European invention, and had been since antiquity, a place of romance, exotic beings, haunting memories and landscapes, remarkable experiences."[10] Neither the East (Orient) nor the West (Occident) are monolithic entities; both are complex, ambiguous, and heterogeneous. The Orient consisted – and consists – of the great civilizations to the East of the West: Islam, China, India, and Japan. The West itself was not always 'the West'. The notion of the West as a political entity dates back to the 16th century. Before that, there was Christendom. And it is in the encounters of Christendom and its closest neighbour, Islam, that the origins of Orientalism, and much of its history, can be traced.[11] The Orient was not merely a geographical, but a man-made and cultural, entity. It was essentially a cultural enterprise, an idea, an artificial construction, an imagined reality, and a career. The Orient was created, it was, in the words of Said, 'Orientalized'. The Orient was subjugated by the Western powers at the beginning of the Modern Age. The Western civilization became a yardstick for measuring the Oriental cultures and civilizations. The conceptual category of 'the West' was pitted against the notion of the Orient and the Orient came to signify all that the West was not and some of what the West actually desired.[12] In short, the Western imperialists perceived the Orient in their own way and imposed that image on the Orient. It was a hegemonic pursuit for the legitimising of their political rule and economic exploitation. As explained by Said, "Orientalism is a style of thought based upon an ontological and epistemological distinction made between 'the Orient' and (most of the time) 'the Occident'...... (It was) the corporate institution for dealing with the Orient, dealing with it by making statements about it, authorizing views of it, describing it, by teaching it, settling it, ruling over it: In short, Orientalism was a Western style for dominating, restructuring, and having authority over the Orient." Said adds, "My contention is that without examining Orientalism as a discourse, one cannot possibly understand the enormously systematic discipline by which European culture was able to manage – and even produce – the Orient politically, sociologically, militarily, ideologically, scientifically, and imaginatively during the post-Enlightenment period. Moreover, so authoritative a position did Orientalism have that I believe no one writing, thinking, or acting on the Orient could do so without taking account of the limitations on thought and action imposed by Orientalism. In brief, because of Orientalism, the Orient was not (and is not) a free subject of thought or action." From the beginning of the 19th century until the end of World War II, France and England dominated the Orient and Orientalism; since the World War II, the United States has dominated the Orient and approaches it as France and England once did. As shown by Said, the relationship between Occident and Orient is a relationship of power, of domination, of varying degrees of a complex hegemony, and is quite accurately indicated in the title of K.M. Panikkar's classic, *Asia and Western Dominance*. Orientalism is something more formidable than a mere collection of lies. Orientalism is not an airy European fantasy about the Orient, but a created body of theory and practice in which, for many generations, there has been considerable material investment. Said has studied Orientalism as a dynamic exchange between individual authors and the large political concerns shaped by the three great empires – British, French, American – in whose intellectual and imaginative territory the writing was produced. It is clear that Said's concern with authority does not entail an analysis of what lies hidden in the Orientalist text, but analysis rather of the text's surface, its exteriority to what it describes. Said does not think that this idea can be overemphasized. Orientalism is premised upon exteriority, that is, on the fact that the Orientalist poet or scholar makes the Orient speak, describes the Orient, renders its mysteries plain for and to the West. He is never concerned with the Orient except as the first cause of what he says. What he says and writes, by virtue of the fact that it is said or written, is meant to indicate that the Orientalist is outside the Orient, both as an existential and as a moral fact. Said makes it clear about cultural discourse and exchange within a culture that what is commonly circulated by it is not 'truth', but representations. Said tries also to explain how Orientalism borrowed and was frequently informed by 'strong' ideas, doctrines, and trends ruling the culture. Thus, there was (and is) a linguistic Orient, a Freudian Orient, a Spenglerian Orient, a Darwinian Orient, a racist Orient, and so on. Yet, never has there been such a thing as a pure or unconditional Orient; similarly, never has there been a non-material form of Orientalism, much less something so innocent as an 'idea' of the Orient. Edward Said admits, "...my hybrid perspective is broadly historical and 'anthropological', given that I believe all texts to be worldly and circumstantial in (of course) ways that vary from genre to genre, and from historical period to historical period.... Yet, unlike Michel Foucault, to whose work I am greatly indebted, I do believe in the determining imprint of individual writers upon the otherwise anonymous collective body of texts constituting a discursive formation like Orientalism. The unity of the large ensemble of texts I analyse is due in part to the fact that they frequently refer to each other: Orientalism is after all a system for citing works and authors...Foucault believes that in general, the individual text or author counts for very little; empirically, in the case of Orientalism (and perhaps nowhere else), I find this not to be so. Accordingly, my analyses employ close textual readings whose goal is to reveal the dialectic between individual text or writer and the complex collective formation to which his work is a contribution." While taking into account Said's views, a mention must be made of the personal dimension. In many ways, his study of Orientalism has been an attempt, to use a Gramscian term, 'to make inventory of traces' upon him. In other words, he delves deeper into the meanings of traces from the past and internalises them. While doing so, he goes beyond xenophobic nationalism.

The historiographical perspective of the Orientalists was imperialist. It emphasized the binary opposition between the 'Western self' and the 'Oriental/Indian other'. The Orientalists regarded the Western people as superior, progressive, and industrious, and pictured the Oriental/Indian people as inferior, backward, and lazy. This feeling of superiority is best exemplified by Macaulay's contention: "A single shelf of a good European library is worth the whole native literature of India and Arabia." Commenting on the historiographical perspective of the Orientalists, Ziauddin Sardar says, "Orientalist scholarship had a particular stance on tradition. To begin with, it emphasized ancient over living tradition. It discovered the 'past' of the Orient, a past over which it had more authority and control than the indigenous people .... In India, Orientalists did not only 'discover' the past, but constructed it in a specifically dualistic form; thus, Muslims became foreigners who represented the inauthentic India, while authentic Hindus and their indigenous civilization had to suffer the oppression of the intruders. A new history was fabricated with a Hindu golden age, which fell to the age of tyranny of Muslim invasions .... Such historic and legalistic constructions were used to characterize Oriental societies as despotic by nature. Oriental despotism was a product of the absence of institutions of civil society without which it was not possible to break free from feudalism..... There was thus a total absence of independent institutions to mediate between individuals and the state. Thus, the individual was permanently exposed to the arbitrary rule of the despot. The absence of civic society not only promoted

Oriental despotism, it also ensured that Muslim societies could not develop economically."[13] The academic and cultural pursuits of the Orientalists were not innocent and harmless. For the British 'administrator-historians' in India, writing history was not merely an academic, but mainly a political-administrative and cultural necessity. As showed by Bernard Cohn, the Western scholars aimed at the 'command of language' to create the 'language of command'.[14] Rather, their 'command of' Oriental/Indian languages, literature, law, history, and culture was for creating the language, literature, law, history, and culture 'of command'. As Edward Said says, "The modern Orientalist was, in his view, a hero rescuing the Orient from the obscurity, alienation, and strangeness which he himself had properly distinguished..., having transported the Orient into modernity, the Orientalist could celebrate his method, and his position, as that of a secular creator, a man who made new worlds as God had once made the old."[15] The Orientalists claimed to have given history to the non-historical Orient. For them, history was one of the instruments of creating their cultural hegemony over the Orient. Through their historiographical pursuits, they underestimated and ridiculed the Orientals/Indians and tried to create divisions among them. The translations of Oriental classics like *Shakuntala* shrouded in Victorian values, James Mill's periodization of Indian history in the Hindu period, the Muslim period, and the British Period, and Grant Duff's 'forest-fire theory' pertaining to the rise of the Marathas are the best examples of this attitude. Using the words of Gauri Viswanathan, one can say that the history written by the Orientalists was a 'mask' of their 'conquest'[16] and hegemony. A strong reaction to the Orientalist historiography came in the form of the nationalist historiography in India. The recent studies do not accept the Hegelian and Marxist models of 'stagnant Indian society'. The 'Eighteenth Century Debate' is a very significant development in this respect.[17]

A number of scholars have made a critique of the Orientalism-thesis of scholars such as Edward Said and Bryan Turner.[18]

The contribution of the Chicago School in this context is worth mentioning. The monolithic presentation of Orientalism and the essentialist approach implied in the concept of 'binary opposition' have been criticized. The postmodernist, the subaltern and the feminist schools have also put forward their arguments forcefully. Kate Currie's book, *Beyond Orientalism,* reviews all such trends brilliantly.[19] As shown by Ziauddin Sardar, after retrenching itself in scholarship and literary imagination, Orientalism has moved on to conquer film, television, and CD-ROMs.[20] The 'mega-theme' and the 'meta-discourse' of Orientalism will certainly continue to stimulate historiographical and cultural discussions and debates.

Notes

1. Sir William Jones (1746-1794): An eminent Sanskrit scholar, who translated Kalidasa's *Shakuntala* into English (1789); the Founder of the Asiatic Society of Bengal (1784); known as 'undisputed founder of Orientalism' (A.J. Arberry's phrase). His ambition was 'to know India better than any other European ever knew it'.
2. Charles Wilkins (1749-1836): A company official and scholar who first translated the *Bhagvad Geeta* into English (1784).
3. Henry Thomas Colebrooke (1765-1837): the founder of the Royal Asiatic Society (1823).
4. Friedrich Max Muller (1823-1900): A German Sanskritist.
5. The pro-capitalism 'laissez faire' principle was the economic counterpart of these two doctrines. This principle, put forward by Adam Smith in his *Wealth of Nations* (1776), greatly influenced British imperialist policy. Jeremy Bentham (1748-1832), who belonged to Smith's school of 'classical economics', is known as the 'father of utilitarianism'. The impact of utilitarianism in India was felt mainly on the revenue system, judicial system and education.
6. Edward W. Said: great authority on Orientalism. An Arab Protestant-Christian Palestinian born in Jerusalem (1935), which was under British control. Educated in Lebanon, Egypt, and the US, taught English and Comparative Literature in American universities.

Contributed two important works on Orientalism: (1) *Orientalism* (1978) and (2) *Culture and Imperialism* (1993). His highly acclaimed overview of Western attitudes towards the Orient has become one of the canonical texts of cultural studies. Died in New York on September 25, 2003.

7. Cited in Edward W. Said, *Orientalism*, (with new Afterword), Penguin Books, New Delhi, 2001, p. 341.
8. Ibid., pp. 16-17.
9. Kate Currie, *Beyond Orientalism*, K. P. Bagchi & Company, Kolkata, 1996, p. 11.
10. Said's views cited in this paragraph are taken from: Said, op. cit., Introduction, pp. 1-28.
11. Ziauddin Sardar, *Orientalism,* Viva Books Pvt. Ltd, New Delhi, 2002, p. 2.
12. Ibid., p. 3.
13. Ibid., pp. 7-8.
14. 'The Command of Language and the Language of Command', Bernard S. Cohn, *Colonialism and its Forms of Knowledge,* Oxford University Press, New Delhi, 1997.
15. Said, op. cit., p. 121.
16. Gauri Viswanathan, *Masks of Conquest: Literary Study and British Rule in India*, Faber and Faber, London, 1990.
17. See for the details:
    Seema Alavi, *The Eighteenth Century in India*, Oxford University Press, New Delhi, 2002.
18. Bryan Turner: author of the books, *Weber and Islam* (1974) and *Marx and the End of Orientalism* (1978), about whom Kate Currie says, "Turner, like Said, centres his analysis of Orientalist constructions on what he designates as the Middle East (West Asia) and North Africa. In part, Turner's work at the time was a neo-Althusserian critique of Hegelian Marxism, in part a 'work of personal decolonisation'... from his earlier Weberian Orientalist heritage." Currie, op. cit., pp. 11-12.
19. Also see the critique of Said's thesis in Sardar, op. cit., Chapter IV.
20. Ibid., Preface, p. vii. For details, see Chapter 5: 'The Postmodern Future'.

4

The Materialist Conception of History

Chhaya Goswami

A concept conceived of as 'metahistory' in the system of thinkers such as Hegel and Marx offers a field of speculation in human society. Since metahistory treats historical evidence in terms of a preconceived pattern, formal analysis, and universal classification, a Marxist approach to historical writing produces history, philosophy, and the social sciences in a new synthesis. Here, mankind is considered as a social being rather than merely a biological being. Furthermore, Marxism explains ideology as the viewpoint of the materialistic society. In Marx's formulation,

> In the social production of their life, men enter into definite relations that are indispensable and independent of their will, relations of production, which correspond to a definite stage of development of their material productive forces. The sum total of these relations of production constitutes the economic structure of society, the real foundation, on which rises a legal and political superstructure and to which follow definite forms of social consciousness.

In this view, ideology has its source, not just in material life, but also in the outlook of the dominant class. According to the Marxists, whenever any changes or clashes occur in this material development, there emerges ideological revolution along with a social revolution.

What is Socialism?

Socialism visualizes a form of society which results from the overthrow of the capitalist system. However, no society can be socialist before going through the stage of capitalism. It is capitalism which creates the conditions for the growth of a socialist movement and ideology and eventually for building a socialist society.

The early socialist thinkers are known as the Enlightenment thinkers of the 18th century. In fact, socialism was not only a product of capitalism, but also a product of the intellectual heritage of the 18th century Enlightenment. They saw history from the perspective of the interest of those who were oppressed. They opposed capitalism and private property as a source of profit. Therefore, they wanted a common or social ownership of means of production. That is why they were called socialists. The type of socialist theory developed by Owen, Saint Simon, Fourier, and Proudhon has been described as 'utopian'. It laid stress on the moral badness of capitalism and the moral goodness of socialism, but its propounders did not know how to bring about this new kind of society, and so they were called utopian socialists. Lenin summed up utopian socialism very aptly in his 'Three Sources and Three Components of Marxism', in which he said:

> It criticised capitalist society, it condemned and damned it, it dreamed of its destruction, it had visions of a better order and endeavoured to convince the rich of the immorality of oppression. But utopian socialism could not indicate the real solution. It could not explain the real nature of wage slavery under capitalism, it could not reveal the laws of capitalist development, or show what social force is capable of becoming the creator of a new society.

Thus, it was left to Karl Marx and Friedrich Engels to provide a new interpretation to socialism, which is better known as scientific socialism or Marxism. However, Marx and Engels were not the only socialists to adopt the realistic as opposed to the rationalistic, utopian, view of the state. Scholars such as Louis Blanc and Lorenz Von Stein, though not socialists, directed their thinking along the line of historical realism. But Marx and Engels were the first socialists to insist that the success of socialism depended on a thorough grasp of the significance of social movements by the proletariat itself, on its realization of its 'historical initiative'.

Marxism

To understand how the Marxist approach is incorporated in history writing, it is essential to understand what the concept of socialism means. A world free from oppression with a society which is organized on the principle of equality and in which the resources of the world are equally shared is the world of socialism. The ideas of such people are known as socialist ideas, and the kind of society they wanted to build is known as a socialist society. Their movements which were aimed at building a socialist society are known as socialist movements.

Karl Marx [1818-1883] based his ideas of how to change the world on a scientific analysis of society through history. He saw the final stage of man's history as a stage in which the society would be communist. He also showed how it could be brought about. Therefore, to distinguish his ideas from those of other socialists, his followers began to call themselves communists, and his ideas began to be known as Marxism.

The first principle of Marxism is determinism because it emphasizes that laws, which the human mind can recognise or determine, govern history. This principle is the foundation of Marxism, on which it has built the socialist creed. Secondly, Marxism stresses on the materialistic approach towards social change. This is because Marx believed that economic growth is basic to social change. Ideas and institutions, laws and politics, and even religion and art are greatly affected by economic factors. In an ever-growing industrial set-up, only the community at large will be able to provide the organizational framework for production. In other words, the means of production must be nationalized.

Marxism refers to the ideas of scientific socialism, which developed in the second half of the 19th century in Europe. Philosophically, Marxism meant a materialist outlook on life and history, i.e. the way in which people produce their requirements of life and the way in which they organize their labour to do it, determines the way they build society and political structure and, ultimately, also the way they think. Applied to man's history, Marxism showed that what decided a particular stage of history was the prevailing mode of production, i.e. the forces of production and the relations of production in a society. The driving and underlying causes of historical development and change were not the changing ideas of human beings, but class struggle. Class struggle, in turn, was the result of the fact that some sections of people or classes were the privileged and ruling classes, and the ruled classes were unprivileged and oppressed. Class struggle was inevitable in history as long as private property existed, i.e. it was an essential part of every stage of historical development till the socialist revolution, when the resources would be collectively owned. These ideas constituted 'historical materialism'.

Based on these ideas, they showed how each society passed through the same stages of development – primitive communism, slavery, feudalism, capitalism, socialism – and how, though some features might be different in different countries, it was not possible to skip any of these stages.

According to Marx, important historical progress is achieved through a conflict between an old and new principle of social organization. This idea originates from concept of dialectics, where discussion involves thesis and antithesis to produce synthesis. Marx viewed that there was always a clash of interests among social groups, which he called class struggle. He called this class struggle the great motivating power of history. There is a close connection between class struggle and the dialectic as a tool of analysis. Marxism regards history as the development of man's effort to master the forces of nature and means of production. History is the succession of changes in social systems and also the development of human relations geared to productive activity.

Marxism: Political Theory

Marx and Engels pointed out that capitalism itself creates the conditions for the overthrow of the capitalist society. Firstly, they showed that capitalism would inevitably be faced with periodic crises of overproduction and underconsumption, and the irreconcilability of the interests of the capitalist and the worker. This is also the main contradiction of capitalism. In order to obtain more profit, the capitalist pays as little as possible to the workers, but in order to sell his products, the worker must have more money to buy, i.e. he must pay them more because they have no other source of income. Obviously, he cannot do both at the same time. For a time, capitalism can overcome these crises by searching for new markets, i.e. colonies, or by waging wars for the re-division of markets, or by taking over some welfare measures for the workers to appease them. But this cannot go on endlessly because the contradiction lies in the system itself. Therefore, from the economic analysis of capitalism, Marx and Engels drew the political conclusion that the overthrow of capitalism was inevitable.

The class, which they said would overthrow this system was the working class or proletariat. Since this class owns nothing except the ability to work and earn in the fight against capitalism, it has 'nothing to lose, except its chains'. Further, to live a meaningful life, it is a necessary task for the proletariat to fight the system. Marx and Engels pointed out that with the emancipation of the working class would come the emancipation of all other sections of society, as it was the working class which formed the lowest layer of this society. Thus, Marx and Engels arrived at the political conclusion that it was the working class which would lead the struggle and be the vanguard of the socialist revolution.

Theory of Revolution

Marx pointed out that in the history of human society through the ages, people have gained nothing without a fight for it, and nothing has been given up by the privileged section of society. Therefore, the emancipation of the working class can come only through their struggle with the capitalist class.

But can this struggle be peaceful? To this, Marx had this to say:

> The entire armed forces and the state machinery are in the hands of the ruling class and they use them precisely for protecting their dominance. There cannot be a peaceful transformation from capitalism and socialism. The working class has to capture state power by revolution and guarantee the building of a socialist state by creating a new state, which will be the dictatorship of the proletariat.

According to Marx, this would not be only an economic fight, and though the working class be the motivating social force for revolution, other sections would also participate. Because of the latter's origins, however, their role would be secondary.

Marx has been severely criticized for denying the influence of any, except the economic factor in history. Unfortunately, Marx perpetuated the mistaken notion that India was a stagnant, historical land. He described India as being caught in what he called the 'Asiatic mode of production'. He posited that India was trapped in a stagnant, unhistorical economic state in which 'Oriental despots' wielded unchanging, absolute power and governed self-sufficient villages. His analysis was flawed perhaps because he was not much acquainted with the actual economic conditions prevailing in India during his time, or of the numerous causes that underlay them.

The controversies surrounding this theory need not be rehashed here; an extensive critique of this theory has been undertaken by Hindess and Hirst, who concluded that "the notion of an 'Oriental' form of state is the product of Western political ideologies and Western attempts to give the East an essential and alien culture different in every respect from the West. The same concepts apply to the Orient and the Occident."

To a certain extent, the Marxist historians who have continued this line of enquiry have perpetuated the outdated and Orientalist notion of India as frozen in time, passive vis-à-vis the active and liberating agency of the West.

Indian History Writings and Marxism

In the writing of history [historiography], the differences in interpretation give rise to different 'schools of history', distinguishable from one another in terms of trend and interpretation. Here, the focus of discussion would be on how the materialistic approach was applied to Indian history by historians.

To begin with, between 1853 and 1857, Marx himself wrote twenty-three articles on India, and Engels eight, bearing on British rule in India. Marx took the 'Eurocentric' view of India's past. He shared all his assumptions on India with the British rulers. Britain was to lay the foundations of the material progress in India on the annihilation of the traditional Indian society. He wrote in 1853:

> Indian society has no history at all, at least no known history. What we call its history is but the history of the successive intruders who founded their empires on the passive basis of that unresisting and unchanging society. The question, therefore, is not whether the English had a right to conquer India, but whether we are to prefer India conquered by the Turk, by the Persian, by the Russian, to India conquered by the Briton.

England had to fulfil a double mission in India, one destructive and the other regenerating – the annihilation of the old Asiatic society and the laying of the material foundations of Western society in Asia. The Arabs, Turks, Tartars, and Mughals, who had successively overrun India, soon became Hinduised, the barbarian conquerors being, by an eternal law of history, themselves conquered by the superior civilization of their subjects. According to Marx, the British were the first conquerors who were superior, and therefore beyond conquest by Hindu civilization. They destroyed it by breaking up the native communities, by uprooting the native industry, and by levelling all that was great and elevated in the native society. The pages in history of their rule in India report hardly anything beyond that destruction. "The work of regeneration hardly transpires through a heap of ruins. Nevertheless, it has begun." Indian Marxists accept this thesis and fully subscribe to it.

Materialistic Conception of Ancient Indian History

Post-independence India has produced a large number of renowned historians. They are easily divisible into two groups – those who carried on the nationalist tradition of the pre-independence period, and those who developed the theory and tools of the Marxist approach to Indian historiography.

A.L. Basham's writings inaugurate a new trend in interpretation. His book, *The Wonder That Was India* (1951), describes various facets of ancient Indian culture. It was he who brought about the shift from political to non-political history. This shift is seen in D.D. Kosambi's work, *An Introduction to the Study of Indian History* (1957), later popularized in *The Culture and Civilization of Ancient India in Historical Outline* (1965). Kosambi, the acknowledged father of Marxist history writing in India, began a new trend in Indian history by adopting the materialist interpretation of history. His writings, influenced by the writings of Karl Marx, present the history of ancient Indian society, economy, and culture in terms of the growth of the forces and relations of production. His work is the first of its kind to show the phases of social and economic progress in terms of tribal and class processes. Criticism of his work came from many quarters, including Basham, yet his book is referred to widely.

Romila Thapar is rightly regarded as an acknowledged authority on Ancient India, who applied the combined methods of Kosambi and made a significant contribution to freeing the history of early India from the tight grip of the dynastic model. No aspect of life has remained untouched by her pen, which is prolific in its productions. Though she is taken to be a Marxist historian, her interpretation is nowhere guided solely by the theory of economic determinism.

B.N. Datta [*Studies in Indian Social Polity*] was the first Marxist historian to refer to the growth of feudalism in early India. After that, it was only in late 1950s and 1960s that the discussion of the problem gained momentum, as is evident from the writings of Kosambi and R.S. Sharma. Following them, a number of Marxist historians, notably B.N.S. Yadav, have made important contributions to this discussion. The school of Marxist historians has equated the feudal phenomenon with a mode of production based on 'feudal rent', which subsumes the existence of a class of landlords, a basic class of producers, with a special connection with the land.

The first significant contribution to the study of ancient Indian religions from a Marxist point of view came from a philosopher, Debi Prasad Chattopadhyaya. His study of ancient Indian materialism, as reflected in its religion and philosophy, has strongly influenced the attitude of some of the historians towards the Indian religious tradition. Likewise, Suvira Jaiswal's monograph on the early Indian history of Vaisnavism (1967) is perhaps the only major Marxist work of significance which purports to study religious phenomenon in the overall milieu of a material setting without overlooking the historical perspective. While Marxist scholar N.N. Bhattacharya emphasizes the equation of women, earth, and the origin of agriculture in his work, historians like Kosambi, R.S. Sharma, and Daniel Thorner bring peasants into the study of Indian history for the first time.

To name a few more writers who seem to have been influenced by the materialistic conception of history, we have A.N. Bose [*Social and Rural Economy of Northern India*], and S.A. Dange [*India from Primitive Communism to Slavery*].

Moreover, in spite of their sharing a common outlook, these writers not only differ on the dating of literary sources such as the *Arthashastra* of Kautilya and the *Jatakas*, they also differ fundamentally on several questions. While some hold that ancient Indian society was a slave society, others argue that this is not true in the same sense as in the case of other ancient societies. Again, while some argue that *varna* corresponds to the Marxist conception of economic class, others think that economic considerations cut across the hereditary social *varnas*. Consequently, it appears that Marxist historiography on ancient India has varying shades of materialist interpretation.

Marxist Historians on Mediaeval India

European and Indian writers set about reconstructing the history of mediaeval India on the basis of chronicles accessible in Persian, Arabic, and Hindi, but mainly in Persian. The study of mediaeval Indian history in modern times may be said to have begun about a century ago when, in the 1860s, and under the patronage of the Asiatic Society of Bengal, the Indo-Persian chronicles of the mediaeval period began to be printed in the Bibliotheca Indica Series. In 1867-77 appeared Elliot and Dowson's *History of India as Told by Its Own Historians*. The original Persian works were so eulogistic of the cruelties of Muslim conquerors and rulers that the great painstaking scholar, Elliot, and his followers were perforce constrained to be critical of mediaeval Indian rulers. This school held the ground for quite some time.

Soon, other writers, who would not agree with this criticism, or who were determined to refute it, appeared on the scene, and the situation so created divided the modern Indian writers on mediaeval history into 'objective' and pro-Muslim or 'apologist' historians.

In the beginning, mediaeval historiography remained confined to political history or biography writing. Then, gradually, the non-political features of mediaeval India, like the cultural influence of Muslim rule, Islam as a civilization, literature and art, and social and economic life, began to attract the attention of scholars. There is now the conviction that history is a form of critical enquiry into the past and not merely a repetition of testimony and authority. The modern historiographer of mediaeval history tries to probe into the ideas behind human actions performed in the past. The writings of Muhammed Habib reflect the influence of progressive civilization. In his introduction to a reprint of Elliot and Dowson's *History of India*, Habib observes that this volume is based upon "the principles of historical materialism developed to suit the conditions of the East and in particular India". The significant feature of Professor Habib's Marxist interpretation of mediaeval Indian history is not that Marxism has absorbed Islam, but that Islam has absorbed Marxism. Habib believed in drastic surgery with Marxian tools to restore the health of a sick society. The idea has caught on and there is a clear Marxist influence on the Aligarh school of history writing, and it has been carried forward by Irfan Habib.

Irfan Habib, in his sagacious study of the Mughal empire, explained the cause of Mughal decline in fiscal terms. He argues that the revolts, which took the shape of peasant uprisings, were the products of economic oppression caused by the proliferation of Mansabdars and exorbitant Mughal revenue exactions. However, the occurrence of these revolts in relatively prosperous regions, and the zamindar leadership that propelled them, makes Habib's exploitation-poverty-resistance causal chain untenable. He denied that the Mughal empire had any potentialities for capitalistic development, despite a considerable presence of commodity production.

The other effort was directed to establishing what the later mediaeval class structures were like, whether different from those of the earlier period or not. Satish Chandra made an initial attempt to delineate the main features of the Mughal Indian political and social order. The last thesis has been contested by Iqtidar A. Khan (1975), while S. Moosvi has patiently reworked the basic statistics in the *Ain-i-Akbari* on which all work on Mughal economic history must largely rely. M. Athar Ali, emphasizing the centralized nature of Mughal polity and the ethnic and religious compositeness of the nobility, has argued against a thesis of an agrarian crisis in that Empire.

History of Modern India in the Marxist Perspective

In modern Indian history, the school or tradition of history writing which was influential in the late 19th and early 20th centuries, was imperialist historiography. Many intellectual influences coexist in this tradition. For example, evangelism and utilitarianism. Later, a nationalist reaction came in the form of a nationalist approach in historiography. The nationalist school of history emphasized the sentiment of national self-esteem and aimed at building up national unity. Nationalist historiography played an important role in providing the ideological basis of the freedom struggle and in analysing the economic consequences of imperialism. However, the focus of nationalist attention was on external, i.e. imperialist, exploitation of India, not so much on the internal, i.e. class, exploitation and the consequent class conflict within Indian society.

Greater concentration on the latter aspect was the consequence of the influence of the Marxist approach, an influence increasingly evident from the 1940s. Moreover, an economic critique of the British rule was incorporated in this approach.

Locating British imperialism in India in a structural analysis of the world capitalist system further developed it.

Nevertheless, in the early stages, there was no concerted effort by Indian historians to interpret Indian history in Marxist terms. M.N. Roy attempted to give a Marxist interpretation of the Indian National Movement, but in a limited form. Therefore, in the economic history of modern India, Marxists like R.P. Dutt's interpretation is regarded as a substantial Marxist interpretation of Indian history from the earliest times to the rise of British power in India. He developed the basic critique of colonial policies and structures. Since his work, *India Today* (1940/46), there has been considerable writings on the Indian National Movement in the Marxist perspective.

Marxist historians of modern Indian history interpret the history of Indian princely states and their rulers with fresh insights. Discussing the notion of 'anarchy' and 'degeneration' attached to the rulers of early modern India by an examination of the character and nature of the new regional regimes in the 18th century, Bipan Chandra, in his Marxist approach, views Nizam Ul Mulk, Saadat Khan, and Murshid Quli Khan as 'men of a high personal morality'. Bipan Chandra's assessments apart, there is evidence to show that many of these new rulers were capable individuals who possessed eclectic and innovative facets. Marthanda Varma Raja, the ruler of Travancore, was a leading statesman whose achievements in constructing a modern arsenal and munificence in his patronage of arts and literature are well known. The remarkable Rajput ruler, Raja Sawai Jai Singh of Amber, made his scientific proclivities apparent by constructing the Jantar Mantar, by founding Jaipur along scientific principles, erecting observatories with advanced instruments, and by translating major scientific works like Euclid's *Elements of Geometry* in Sanskrit. Ranjit Singh, the ruler of the Sikhs, built a powerful army along European lines and set modern foundries to manufacture cannon.

Marxist historians like to assert that colonialism was a disruptive force. The British conquest of Bengal was not any usual conquest; Bengal served as a springboard for further British expansionism. Plassey was an event that led to the full-blown development of colonialism in the subcontinent. The colonialism that emerged was not only inherently 'alien' in character, but also a product of capitalism. Irfan Habib, discussing the economic changes that British rule initiated, argues that the grant of Diwani in 1765 reduced the bullion flows into India, caused inflation, and intensified the drain of wealth from Bengal and, after 1813, large-scale de-industrialisation constituted a major break with the past.

Irfan Habib and other Indian scholars have argued that India was itself on the threshold of an industrial capitalist revolution that was thwarted by the impact of colonial rule.

Discussing here the early materialistic historical works that influenced other historians of recent time requires mention of the writings of Sumit Sarkar. His works on modern India, *Swadeshi Movement in Bengal 1903-1908; Bibliographical Survey of Social Reform Movements; Modern India 1885-1947; Popular Movements and Middle-Class Leadership in Late Colonial India;* and *Writing Social History* are mainly influenced by the radical social history of the 1960s and 1970s associated with the pattern of Marxist thinking and visions of more democratic and humane forms of socialism.

Today, Marxist historians and writers are well entrenched in the academic and media sectors. The Indian government has encouraged their rise. After partition, Pakistan declared itself a theocratic state as is the case with many Muslim nations. India opted to remain a secular country.

Conclusion

The biggest single achievement of Marxist historiography in India was displacing the dynastic model of viewing the past that originated in the imperialist school of Indian historiography and was taken over with change in emphasis by the nationalist historiographers. Socioeconomic history took centrestage after Kosambi published his seminal works on early India. The only school making a mark after the birth of the Marxist approach is that of the subaltern historians who attempted to construct 'history from below', but their focus is mainly on modern India in contrast with the Marxists, who attempted a materialistic interpretation of the entire course of Indian history. In the end, one may also note that the feminist perspective on Indian history with gender as a category of historical analysis has made a modest beginning in the articles of Uma Chakravarty and Kumkum Roy, though a full-fledged monograph on any aspect for a period of Indian history is yet to manifest itself.

Further Readings

Ali, B. Sheik, *History: Its Theory and Method*, Macmillan, Delhi, 1978.

Crump, C.G., *History and Historical Research*, George Routledge & Sons, London, 1928.

Habib, Irfan, *Essays in Indian History*, Tulika, New Delhi, 1995.

Lett, Gordon, *History and Social Theory*, Merlin Press, London, 1969.

Majumdar, R.C., *Historiography in Modern India*, Asia Publishing House, Mumbai, 1970.

Philips, C.H., (ed.), *Historians of India, Pakistan and Ceylon*, Oxford University Press, London, 1961.

Sally, Graves, *A History of Socialism*, The Hogarth Press, London, 1939.

Sarkar, Sumit, *Writing Social History*, Oxford University Press, New Delhi, 1997.

Sen, S.P., (ed.), *Historians of Historiography in Modern India*, Institute of Historical Studies, Kolhapur, 1973.

Syed, A.J., (ed.), *D.D. Kosambi on History and Society*, A Department of History of the University of Bombay Publication, Mumbai, 1985.

Thakur, V.K., *Historiography of Indian Feudalism*, Commonwealth Publishers, New Delhi, 1989.

Thapar, Romila, *Ancient Indian Social History*, Orient Longman, New Delhi, 1978.

Thapar, Romila, (ed.), *Recent Perspectives of Early Indian History*, Popular Prakashan, Mumbai, 1995.

5

The Annales School

History beyond Traditional Frontiers

Aravind Ganachari

Few groups of scholars have had as great an impact or more fertilizing an effect on the study of history in the 20th century than the French historians of 'the *Annales* School', centred on the École Pratique des Hautes Études in Paris. It is a group of those historians whose regular organ is that periodical originally entitled, *Annales d'histoire Économique et Sociale* and now – that is since 1947 – *Annales: Economies, Sociétés, Civilizations.* The historians of this school, French in origin, French in inspiration, are held by a distinct philosophy and marked by a distinct literary style.

The loyalty of the Annales School is to their three consecutive founding fathers, Marc Bloch (1886-1944), Lucien Fèbvre (1878-1956), and Fernand Braudel (1902-1985). But Braudel himself added the name of Henri Berr (1862-1955) among those who contributed to the origin and programme of this school. Of course, behind these four, lie the names of older scholars who have influenced the four founding fathers: Fustel de Coulanges (1830-1889)[1] in institutional history, François Simiand in economic theory, Emile Durkheim (1858-1917)[2] in sociology, Vidal la Blache (1845-1918)[3] in geography, and no doubt many others, a few of whom were historians themselves.

What is the Philosophy of the Annales School?

The goal of the Annales School from the outset was to undo the work of the Sorbonnistes, to turn the French historians away from the narrowly political and diplomatic history. They believed that the study of the history of France was in doldrums, lagging far behind such history in Germany, England, and the United States. What they saw was the retardation of historical work in France, which they ascribed to an institution, an attitude, and a deficiency. The institution was the Faculty of Letters of the University of Paris, more precisely the dominant historians of that faculty known as the Sorbonnistes. Lucien Febvre regarded the attitude of the Sorbonnistes as a symptom of the shrinking timidity of the France that emerged in a kind of disarray both after the debacle of 1870 and from the Pyrrhic victory in 1914-18. The professors of the History faculty at Sorbonne immersed themselves in political, constitutional, and diplomatic history, harping on the old concept of factual, narrative history. The Annales School believed that the Sorbonnistes produced, to put in J.H. Hexter's words, "very large tomes on very small matters. Worse, as the trainers of succeeding generations of French historians, they produced a progeny in their image...This was a deplorable deficiency, the thinness, the malnutrition that the Historical establishment, forgetting the great tradition of an earlier day, forgetting Guizot, Thierry, and Michelet, was imposing on the study of history in France." Febvre and Bloch believed that these historians turned their back on all the new and exciting horizons that historians in other lands were discovering and exploring.

The main aim of the Annales School was to turn these historians toward the new vistas in history, proclaiming the supremacy of social and economic history, and enlisting the aid of anthropology, climatology, psychology, geography, and any other relevant sister discipline. In the very first volume of the *Annales d'histoire Sociale*, a brief preface – '*a nos lecteurs*' – was published by its '*directeurs*', Marc Bloch and Lucien Febvre, in which they announced their radical design and declared, "History has become sterilized." They sought a divorce between the old historical scholar, applying the sound rules of his craft to the documents of the past, and the new social scientist, adventuring among the economies and societies of the present. Further, they thought that history had become compartmentalized and sub-divided into ancient, mediaeval, and modern, and societies into primitive and civilized. This was considered to be an impediment to the understanding of the living past and also of the living present, since the two are continuous.

Their aim was to create the totality of a society, past or present, to understand its delicate mechanisms, and yet not see it as a machine, but as a living organism with a dynamic of its own. This requires delicate textual scholarship, for the records of the past are texts with their own internal mysteries. The mere course of political events was not to be seen in isolation from the physical and social environment which surrounded and conditioned them, for these are important human activities, and history is, above all, a science of humanity. These activities, like all other human activities, are conditioned by time and place. They are products of a complex of forces which is not easily unravelled because each of them acts and reacts on the other. Man is a social animal and is conditioned by the society in which he lives, as that society, in turn, is conditioned by its geographical and climatic matrix; politics and ideas are limited not only by these external forces, but by the political and intellectual deposits around them.

What the Annales School proclaimed was a history whose scope would extend to embrace all the sciences of man – to the 'globality' of all the human sciences, and which would seize upon them all in some fashion or other to construct its own proper methods and true domain.

This was the *mentalité* of what came to be known as the Annales School of French historians, or the Annalistes. In a sense of the term, this *mentalité* became a *structure*, a controlled habit of thought deeply embedded in the minds of the believers. The historians of the Annales School respected the organic nature of societies, the vitality of man, but they were also rationalists in their method. Whatever could be rationally pursued, measured, calculated, quantified, was so pursued.

Three elements of the Annales School could be emphasized: First, there is the attempt to grasp the totality, and the vital unity, of any historical period or society. Second, there is the conviction that history is at least partly determined by forces which are external to man and yet not entirely neuter or independent of him, nor for that matter, of each other: forces like geography and climate, partly intangible, only intellectually perceptible, and more volatile such as social formations and intellectual traditions. Third, there is the determination, while never losing sight of this totality of human activity, this interdependence of motivating and limiting forces, to reduce the area of comprehension by rigorous statistical analysis of whatever can be analysed, by the measurement of whatever can be measured. In short, to use all the refined techniques of the mathematician, the econometrician, and the statistician.

The Origin

The origin and programme of the Annales School involved three men: Marc Bloch, Lucien Febvre, and Fernand Braudel. It was Braudel who added the name of Henri Berr as the precursor of the Annales.

Henri Berr was a part of the Annales before the journal was created, from 1900, or even from 1890. In his very early years, he was a brilliant pupil with multiple interests and attained many honours in national competitions in 1880-81. He won the Prize of Honour in Rhetoric, first prize in French compositions and also one in philosophy. Three years later, he graduated in Humanities - literature, Latin and Greek. Since 1898, Berr had been a teacher at the Lycée Henry IV. As a philosopher, Berr followed the great intellectual debates of his time, seeking to master them and discover their sense.[4] He took great interest in contributing to the *Revue de Synthèse Historique*, which was founded in 1900. By 1910, the quiet university establishment was already disturbed as much by the ideas discussed in the *Revue* as the fact that Berr had begun to assemble around himself a group of lively, active, enthusiastic, and assertive fringe intellectuals – historians, geographers, economists, sociologists, biologists, anthropologists and, of course, philosophers. These included names such as Henri Hauser, François Simiand, Abel Rey, Paul Lacombe, Paul Mantoux, Lucien Febvre and, later, Marc Bloch. If Berr wrote little, the fact is that his main contribution was to summon, speak, instruct, discuss, listen, bring together, and lose himself in dialogues and innumerable small councils.[5] In 1920, Berr started his monumental collection, *Evolution of Humanity*. He founded in 1925 the *Centre de Synthèse* and a little afterwards, his very famous *Semaines de Synthèse*.

The *Semaines* were the medium for his marvellous activity. In 1933, for instance, the *Semaines* were dedicated to the notions of science and laws of science. It was in the circle set up around Berr between 1900 and 1910, and renewed thereafter, that the desire was born to make a more combative journal than the *Revue de Synthèse*, one that would be less philosophical, but based on concrete new research. That finally gave birth to the *Annales d'histoire Économique et Sociale*. But, the birth was slow. Bloch and Fèbvre met one another at the University of Strasbourg,[6] where they were both appointed in 1919. They waited ten long years to launch their review in 1929. During that long interval, they collaborated regularly with Berr. The announcement of the new review in 1929 made no allusion to the *Revue de Synthèse*. All the same, the creation of the *Annales* in 1929 involved a break – the break between father and son, but the father scarcely complained. The gap between the *Annales* and the *Revue de Synthèse* widened. For Berr, 'society included economies', and the *Annales*, therefore, only cast light upon "an aspect of the life of societies which has long remained obscure, and to which the Marxist drew attention".

The Annalistes, during the first ten years of their existence, were the fruit of a constant collaboration, of an unparalleled friendship, between Lucien Febvre and Marc Bloch. The force of their impact was enhanced by the fact that mediocrity reigned supreme in French historiography and, consequently, almost all of the university was hostile to their entry. Twice Bloch tried to enter the college in Paris, but it was only in 1936 that he was able to enter the Sorbonne in succession to Henri Hauser. Fèbvre entered the college only on his second attempt. By 1936, both of them were at Sorbonne in Paris and thus the centre of their activity shifted from Strasbourg to Paris.

A brief biographical sketch is as follows: Bloch was the son of a great historian, Gustav Bloch, himself a specialist in Roman history, a professor at the École Normale Supérieure and then at the Sorbonne. His son, Marc, a student at the École Normale and a graduate in history, won a fellowship for study in Germany at the Universities of Berlin and Leipzig (1908-9), and then held a post in Paris in the Thiers Foundation. In 1920, in Strasbourg, he published his thesis, *Kings and Serfs: A Chapter in Capetian History*. By 1929, when he took on the editorship of the *Annales*, he had behind him several publications.

A veteran of World War I, called back to military service at the age of fifty-three in 1939, the younger Bloch had seen the collapse of France and of everything in which he believed. His Jewish ancestry made it impossible for him to return to his professorship at the Sorbonne. He took refuge first with the exiled University of Strasbourg at Clermont-Ferrand, then with the University of Montpellier. He could have fled to the United States, but he refused to leave France. He considered himself so thoroughly French, so impregnated with the spirit and tradition of France, that he felt living elsewhere would be suffocating. Under such circumstances he began writing the book, *The Historian's Craft*. But when the Germans crossed the line of demarcation, after the landings in North Africa, Bloch was driven from academic life. He became a member of the Resistance, a leader of the group centring in Lyons. There he was captured by the Germans in the spring of 1944, imprisoned, and cruelly mistreated. On June 16, 1944, as the Nazi hold began to weaken, he was taken from his cell and shot in an open field near Lyons with twenty-six others. The book was never finished,[7] but the fragments were collected and published by Lucien Fèbvre.

Bloch saw life as a whole, as a complicated interplay of ideals and realities, of conscious innovation and unconscious conservation. He said that similar to life, history was a whole, that no period and no topic could be understood, except in relation to other periods and topics. Also, he never made any assumption that economic factors explained all human behaviour and believed that society is held together as much by beliefs and customs, as by economic interests. He was a great practitioner of the new approach to history in another way, in his ability to discover and use new types of source material. Old maps, place names, ancient tools, aerial surveys, folklore – all contributed to his brilliant description of French society during the long centuries when agriculture was the predominant occupation.

Lucien Fèbvre, born in 1878 at Nancy, the capital of Lorraine, was the son of a graduate of the École Normale and a teacher of grammar. A student of the Lycée Louis le Grand and the École Normale, he graduated in history in 1902. Fèbvre was on the staff of the Thiers Foundation in Paris when he came to know Henri Berr, of whom he asked advice while writing his thesis. A socialist or socialistically inclined, Fèbvre was inspired by Lucien Gallois (1857-1941), the geographer, disciple, and friend of Vidal la Blache (whom Fèbvre also knew). And throughout his life, Fèbvre remained a professed geographer, a keen observer of land, plants, men, and countrysides. *The Earth and Human Evolution*, published by him in 1920, is an unparalleled work. His thesis, *Philip II and the Franche Comté*, is a masterpiece and bears the Annales approach much before it was brought into reality in 1929. After Marc Bloch's death in 1944, Fèbvre was in fact the sole editor of the *Annales* until his death in 1956.

Bloch's highly sophisticated studies of the problem of gold in the Middle Ages, of slavery in the Dark Ages, and of the institutional and social character of feudalism studies, in which an intelligence of textual interpretation and modern, non-historical techniques were combined with passionate interest in humanity, opened a new and exciting way. If Bloch applied this philosophy to mediaeval history, Fèbvre applied it to the 'early modern' period: socially and politically in his work on his native Franche Comté, intellectually in his work on Martin Luther and the problem of infidelity in the 16th century.

Fernand Braudel is the third of the founding fathers, the last of the triumvirate, with whose names the Annales School is always associated. Braudel was born in 1902. His father was a teacher in Paris. He studied at the Lycée Voltaire in Paris (1913-20) and received a degree in History from the Sorbonne in 1923. At 21, he taught history in the Lycée at Constantine in Algeria between 1923 and 1932, interrupted only by military service in 1925-26. In 1931, Henri Pirenne spoke at Algiers about his ideas on the closure of the Mediterranean after the Muslim invasions. His lectures proved prodigious and Braudel was subsequently led to choose the Mediterranean as a topic for research.

In 1935, Braudel was offered a position on the faculty at São Paolo in Brazil and lived there until 1937. During the early 1930s, he came in contact with Henri Berr and Lucien Fèbvre. From Brazil, he came back in 1937 to the École des Hautes Etudes. In the summer of 1939, he started writing a book in Febvre's house. Then came the War and Braudel served on the Rhine frontier. From 1940 to 1945, he was a prisoner in Germany, first in Mainz and then in the special camp at Lúbeck. "For prison can be a good school. It teaches patience, tolerance," wrote Braudel at a later date.[8] During his five years in captivity, Braudel wrote his masterpiece, *The Mediterranean*

World in the Age of Philippe II.[9] In 1946, he became a member of the board of directors of *Annales.* In 1949, he succeeded Fèbvre at the College de France and was nominated president of the École des Hautes Études en Sciences Sociale. From Febvre's death in 1956 till 1968, Braudel was the sole editor of the *Annales.* In 1962, he founded the Maison des Sciences de l'Homme, where he was also the principal administrator. His work was appreciated abroad from early on in his career, and he was considered to be one of the greatest historians of his time. In France, however, he received public acclaim only after 1979, when he published *Civilization and Capitalism 15th-18th Century.* In 1984, he was elected to the Académie Françoise. Braudel died in 1985.

Braudel, inspired by the philosophy of his masters, studied the Mediterranean in far greater depth – first geographically, then economically and socially, and finally politically and strategically. His great work moves, rationally and methodologically, from *géo-histoire* to *événementielle.* This required him to look at the Mediterranean Sea, and at the lands which enclosed it, and at the human communities which lived in those lands, bound together – directly or indirectly – by that great unifying inland waterway, as a unity, a unity which, being first geographical, then social, transcended the spectacular political fracture of the 16th century.

As Braudel himself wrote in the preface to his first edition, the work consists of three parts: (1) There is an almost imperceptible history of man in relation to his geographical and climatic environment; (2) There is the more mobile history of social forms, the history of different human groups, some larger than others, but all equally determined by the physical matrix which encloses them; (3) There is the *histoire événementielle*, the history of events, "surface disturbances, crests of foam that the tides of history carry on their strong backs". Such a task is, of course, huge and depends on vast reading in a wide range of disciplines: geography, economics, sociology – indeed, the whole range of human sciences. The central problem he tackled was that of the decline of the Mediterranean, the moment when Europe changed from a Mediterranean to Atlantic economy. Braudel's arguments and conclusions have been constantly fed by new material and new statistics.

For Braudel, all historical work is concerned with breaking down past time, choosing among its chronological realities according to more or less preferences and exclusions. There is an account of conjunctures which lays open large sections of the past, say ten, twenty, fifty years at a stretch, ready for examination. He felt that by concentrating overly on the 'current event' in social studies, something that is practised under the name of empirical sociology, which confines itself to the facts of the short term and makes investigations the sociologist provides myopic and short visions into the understanding of history. To put it in his own words:

> where sociology is concerned, our quarrel along the frontiers of the short term must necessarily be a rather bitter one. Sociological investigations into the contemporary scene seem to run in a thousand different directions, from sociology to psychology to economics, and to proliferate among us as they do abroad. They are, in their own way, a bet on the irreplaceable value of the present moment, with its 'volcanic' heat, its abundant wealth. What good would be served by turning back toward historical time: impoverished, simplified, devastated by silence, reconstructed above all, let's say it again, *reconstructed*.[10]

Therefore, he thought, history was capable of traversing even greater distances, a history to be measured in centuries: 'the history of the long, even of very long time span, of the *longue durée*'. The problem of the *longue durée* was to provide a 'structure', which meant an organization, a coherent and fairly fixed series of relationships between realities and social masses. Some structures, he thought, because of their long life, become stable statements for an infinite number of generations. In this respect, he felt that 'man has been a prisoner of climate, of vegetation, of the animal population, of a particular agriculture, of a whole slowly established balance from which he cannot escape without the risk of everything being upset'. The same element of permanence also exists in the domain of cultural affairs. However, Braudel was fully aware of the methodological problems and complications such an attitude posed. It meant becoming used to a slower tempo, which 'sometimes borders on the motionless'. Despite the shortcomings, he argued, it is in relation to these expanses of slow-moving history that the whole of history is to be rethought, as if on the basis of an infrastructure. Braudel deftly used these ideas in all his works.

An equally fascinating work of Braudel in pursuance of the Annales paradigm is *Civilization & Capitalism - 15th-18th Century*.[11] He intended in this work the uncovering of unusual themes, 'which must be incorporated into a coherent history, the assembling of a number of '*parahistoric* languages' - demography, food, costume, lodging, technology, money, towns - which are kept separate from each other and which develop in the margin of traditional history.[12] He, thus, introduced everyday life into the domain of history. To put it in his own words:

> Everyday life consists of the little things one hardly notices in time and space. The more we reduce the focus of vision, the more likely we are to find ourselves in the environment of material life: the broad sweep usually corresponds to History with a capital letter, to distant trade routes, and the network of national and urban economies... The event is, or is taken to be, unique; the everyday happening is repeated, and the more often it is repeated, the more likely it is to become a generality or rather a structure. It pervades society at all levels, and characterizes ways of being and behaving which are perpetuated through endless ages...

Braudel has touched on uncommon topics for historical scrutiny, of which a few examples can be cited as illustrations. He infers that fashion is the product of a growth in wealth, of a shift in emphasis from heredity to wealth and talent, of a modification and ultimate abolition of estate societies, of a change in values from age to youth. He explains how the costumes of the Italian Renaissance receded during the 16th century before the sombre hues of mighty Spain and how the colourful costumes of the rising French then encroached on the Spanish domain. Fashion denotes, on the one hand, a distinctive creation and, on the other, a multiplication of material goods and other cultural traits, a transformation of luxuries into needs. He observes that every culture or civilization creates its own special order of cultural relationships. He demonstrates that the transmission of new cultural traits was a factor of expanding wealth. It was probably also a consequence of a resulting preference for material goods over social stability. For two reasons, he stated, poor societies prefer the comfort of social solidarity to the pleasures of material objects: Firstly, abundance and extravagance tend to attract the envy and wrath of the privileged and the puissant, and secondly, in an economic sense, the poor are less able to afford change than the rich.

Among the European innovations subject to Braudel's scrutiny are the modern apartment, in which every room serves a particular purpose, and in which the privacy of the bedroom is virtually guaranteed; individual forks, spoons and plates; the printing press and the printed book; mirrors and window glass. In terms of material goods, as of ideas and mental structures or mindsets, there was thus a shift, he points out, in early modern Europe toward a valuation of the individual. Braudel shows keen awareness of complexities such as a simultaneous growing esteem for material goods and a regression in cleanliness.[13] Lastly, Braudel turns his attention to money: metallic money, money of account, paper money, and instruments of credit. One of the objects of the conquest of the sea, he observed, was the appeasement of 'a hunger for gold'. In this way, he laid one of the psychological foundations of capitalism.

However, Braudel's methodology and approach have been subjected to historical criticism. The critics have admiringly felt that volume one's 'material life' – demography, diet, costume, lodging, and technological resources, as well as the varying patterns of town life, luxury goods, and monetary operations – remains the most thought-provoking portion of the work because it pulls together into an economic perspective a galaxy of topics normally left untouched by economic historians and treated disjointedly by social historians or cultural historians. Despite its enormity, Braudel has been criticized for his notion of capitalism, the history of European prices, and other such related issues. He is condemned continually "to resort to illustrations more than to analysis, to exhibit more than to critical interpretation, and in sum to argument which stands and falls with the soundness of others' research. Partly as a consequence of this, Braudel's desire for totality of content sacrifices precision to inconclusiveness. His book is marvellous for raising problems; it offers a galaxy of fascinating specificities. But it jumps from the specific to the general with the vaguest of theoretical allusions."[14]

Notwithstanding the criticism, Braudel has been held as one of the towering historians of the 20th century, an epitome of the Annales paradigm, one who influenced succeeding generations of historians to evolve an inter-disciplinary approach to historical study, and one who saw the past beyond the traditional frontiers of history.

In the tradition of the Annales School, thought Fernand Braudel, it was appropriate for him to hand over the management to young men: Jacques Le Goff, a mediaevalist; Emmanuel Le Roy-Ladurie, a modernist; and Marc Ferro, a specialist in Russian history. He wrote, "I have found myself directly disagreeing with them. But thanks to them, the old dwelling has become a house of youth once more." (How many of our own historians would accept this?)

Notes

1. Fustel de Coulanges, French historian and author of *The Ancient City* and *History of the Institutions of Ancient France* (in six volumes).
2. Émile Durkheim, French social theorist, who was one of the pioneers in the development of human sociology.
3. Vidal la Blache, French geographer, who stressed the effects of geography on history. His best known work is *Tableau de la Géographie de la France*, first published in 1903 as an introduction to a history of France by Ernest Lavisse and later published separately. He taught at Nancy and Paris, where he founded the periodical *Annales de Géographie.*
4. The title of Henri Berr's his thesis speaks for itself: *Synthesis of Knowledge and of History: Essay on the Future of History.*
5. After 5 p.m. everyday, Berr opened his doors to visitors, preferably at his office at 2 Rue Villeboi-Mareuil. He was above all good company, a man of intelligence, prepared and skilful in talk.
6. The University of Strasbourg was founded in 1919.
7. Marc Bloch dedicated this unfinished book to Lucien Fèbvre in 1941.
8. Braudel wrote, "It was in captivity that I wrote that enormous work, sending school copy book after school copy book to Lucien Fèbvre. Only my memory permitted this tour de force. Had it not been for my imprisonment, I would surely have written quite a different book."
9. The French title is *La Méditerranéen et lé Monde Méditerranéen á l''Epoque de Philippe II.* It was published in 1949 and its English translation was published in 1972-73. Its main outline was already determined, if not entirely written by 1939, at the close of the early dazzling period of the Annales School, of which it is the direct result. The book itself is laid ceremoniously at the feet of Lucien Fèbvre. The text is exactly 1,100 pages long, followed by a bibliography of 28 pages detailing, among other matters, intensive research in archives located in 19 repositories in 11 cities in four countries. The first part is of 304 pages, the second part of 414 pages, and the third of 366 pages.
10. Fernand Braudel, 'History and the Social Sciences – The *Longue Durée*', in Maurice Aymard and Harbance Mukhia (eds.), *French Studies in History, Vol. Inheritance,* Orient Longman, New Delhi, 1988. p. 81.
11. The early version of the first volume appeared in French in 1967 under the title, *Civilisation Matérielle et Capitalisme (XVe-XVIIIe*

Siécle). This was translated into English by Mariam Kochan in 1973 under the title, *Capitalism and Material Life, 1400-1800.* It was extensively revised by Braudel, and turned into three volumes: *The Structures of Everyday Life*; *The Wheels of Commerce*; and *The Perspective of the World.*

12. Braudel has mentioned this in the Preface to the first volume, *The Structures of Everyday Life.*
13. Braudel writes that the closing down during the 16th century of public baths, which were reputed to be breeding places of epidemics and of syphilis, and the discontinuance of private baths, were attended by a growing use of musk, ambergris, lavender, violet, rose, iris and other strong scents.
14. Samuel Kinser, 'Capitalism Enshrined: Braudel's Triptych of Modern Economic History' in *The Journal of Modern History*, No.4, December 1981.

Further Readings

Braudel, Fernand, *Civilization & Capitalism - 15th-18th Century*, Vol. 1: *The Structures of Everyday Life*; Vol. 2: *The Wheels of Commerce*; Vol. 3: *The Perspective of the World*, Phoenix Press Paperback, London, 2002 (First published by William Collins in 1981).

—, 'History and the Social Sciences - The *Longue Durée*', in Maurice Aymard and Harbance Mukhia (eds), *French Studies in History Vol. Inheritance,* Orient Longman, New Delhi, 1988.

Hobsbawm, Eric, 'British History and the Annales', in *On History*, Abacus, 1997, pp. 236-45.

Kinser, Samuel, 'Annales Paradigm: The Geo-Historical Structuralism of Fernand Braudel', in *American Historical Review,* No. 86, February 1981.

—, 'Capitalism Enshrined: Braudel's Triptych of Modern Economic History', in *The Journal of Modern History*, No. 4, Vol. 53, December 1981.

6

Structure and Discourse

Reading the 'Political Unconscious' of History

Jatin Wagle

While discussing the relationship between structuralism and the philosophy of social sciences, Jean Piaget claims that in our analyses of social formations, if we opt 'for structure and devalue genesis, history and function, or even the very activity of the *subject* itself', we would enter into conflict with what he describes as 'the dialectical modes of thought'.[1] Two of the obvious assumptions couched in this statement are that structuralism, with its emphasis on structure, devalues history and the human subject, and also that structuralism and Marxism are incommensurable theoretical approaches. The obvious merit of Piaget's formulation notwithstanding, we find that there is a rich intellectual force field that holds all these seemingly oppositional elements together. It seems to us that such constellations of ideas, including structure, history, and Marxism, have been and continue to be creative and significant influences on historiography and hermeneutics.[2] It is the task of this paper to deal with some of the more seminal questions regarding history and historiography raised by Althusserian structuralist Marxism and the early writings of Foucault, as they are found inflected in a Jamesonian critique, in the context of literary and cultural studies.[3]

Before the Althusserian discussion of history, it needs to be mentioned that the dominant strains within structuralism were primarily concerned with the developments in linguistics and their broad relevance and application to areas such as literary and culture studies and anthropology, and for Althusser, these were, broadly speaking, instances of what he called structuralist ideology. Thus, we can describe structuralism as a methodology or theory that takes as its object of investigation a 'system' – the complex web of relations between a grouping of facts, rather than facts as isolated entities. According to Piaget, the basic concepts of structuralism are totality,[4] self-regulation, and transformation. While defining structuralism 'negatively', he says that it is opposed to compartmentalization, i.e. the study of facts as discrete objects unconnected with one another, and diachronic study, i.e. the examination of facts as they develop across time. Instead, structuralism recommends a synchronic study of systems, i.e. the immanent examination of structures as though the temporal frame had been frozen. While defining structuralism 'positively', Piaget claims that it rests on the belief that structures are self-sufficient and intrinsically intelligible, and to grasp them, we do not need to make extraneous references, and secondly, that structures in general, notwithstanding their specific differences, have common, universal characteristics.[5]

While describing the role of structuralism in social sciences, Piaget discusses its best-known precinct, the structuralist anthropology of Claude Levi-Strauss. Levi-Strauss' 'analytical' structuralism, claims Piaget, seeks to explain empirical systems by postulating the 'deep' structures from which these systems derive – the 'conceptual structure' behind the 'concrete' social relations.[6] Maurice Godelier, the Marxist anthropologist much influenced by Levi-Strauss, suggests that for Levi-Strauss, as for Marx, "structures are not directly visible or observable realities, but levels of reality which exist beyond man's visible relations and whose functioning constitutes the deeper logic of a social system".[7] In this context, Levi-Strauss defends a synchronic study of societies, as he claims that the changes brought about by history do not affect the structure of the human mind. However, he assigns a vital, but rather limited, role to history, as to his mind, it needs to be transcended[8] by a structuralist theory:

> (History) proves indispensable for cataloguing the elements of any structure whatever, human or non-human, in their entirety. It is, therefore, far from being the case that the search for intelligibility comes to an end in history as though this were its terminus. Rather, it is history that serves as the point of departure in any quest for intelligibility.... history leads to everything, but on the condition that it be left behind.[9]

It is quite clear here that though Levi-Strauss appears to curtail the role of what is conventionally understood as history, he is in fact broadening the scope of what can be described as a theory of history that investigates 'the forms of the mind'. In this context, it is striking that Levi-Strauss characterizes his task as that of evolving "a system of schemata intercalated between Marxian 'infrastructures and superstructures'."[10]

> Marxism, if not Marx himself, has too commonly reasoned as though practices followed directly from praxis. Without questioning the undoubted primacy of infrastructures, I believe that there is always a mediator between praxis and practices,[11] namely, the conceptual scheme by the operation of which matter and form, neither with any independent existence, are realized as structures, that is as entities which are both empirical and intelligible. It is to this theory of superstructures, scarcely touched upon by Marx, that I hope to make a contribution.[12]

According to Jameson, this claim needs to be treated seriously, as Marxism itself has perceived ideology rather crudely as a form of masking or mystification, or as conscious class distortion, and has failed to present a truly systematic investigation of the superstructures.[13]

This brings us to the complex and contentious terrain of the structuralist Marxist conception of history. We could begin with Althusser's proposition for the task of historiography, modified and recommended by Fredric Jameson for the enterprise of literary history: 'not to elaborate some achieved and lifelike simulacrum of its supposed object, but rather to 'produce' the latter's 'concept'.'[14] Althusser's creative rereading of Marx and his rewriting of the history of Marxism appear to follow this dictum. He claimed that despite the superficial similarities between the writings of early and later Marx, they were two distinct modes of thought. The *problematiques*, i.e. the underlying theoretical/epistemological structures of each of them, was so different that it could be called incommensurable. He detected an 'epistemological break', around 1845, between Marx's early Hegelian and later scientific formulations through a 'symptomatic reading' that analysed the visible symptoms of the discourse to reveal the underlying *problematique*.[15]

However, the central argument of Althusserian historiography can be found in Althusser's theory of the three historical forms of causality or effectivity. This seminal statement also delineates his reassessment of the Marxian infrastructure-superstructure model as a structural – and not an expressive – totality, and it is best read in his own words:

> The epistemological problem posed by Marx's radical modification of political economy can be expressed as follows: by means of what concept is it possible to think of the new type of determination, which has just been identified as the determination of phenomena of a given region by the structure of that region? ... In other words, how is it possible to define the concept of structural causality? ... very schematically, we can say that classical philosophy... had...only two systems of concepts with which to think effectivity. The mechanistic system, Cartesian in origin, which reduced causality to a *transitive* and analytical effectivity, could not be made to think the effectivity of a whole on its elements... But a second system was available,

one conceived precisely in order to deal with the effectivity of a whole on its elements: the Leibnitzian concept of *expression.* This is the model that dominates all Hegel's thought. But it presupposes in principle that the whole in question be reducible to an *inner essence*, of which the elements of the whole are then no more than the phenomenal forms of expression, the inner principle of the essence being present at each point in the whole, such that at each moment, it is possible to write the immediately adequate equation: such and such element (economic, political, legal, literary, religious, etc., in Hegel) = the inner essence of the whole. Here was a model which made it possible to think the effectivity of the whole on each of its elements, but if this category – inner essence/outer phenomenon – was to be applicable everywhere and at every moment to each of the phenomena arising in the totality in question, it presupposed that the whole had a certain nature, precisely the nature of a 'spiritual' whole in which each element was expressive of the entire totality as a 'pars totalis'. In other words, Leibnitz and Hegel did have a category for the effectivity of the whole on its elements or parts, but on the absolute condition that the whole was not a structure...

(The third concept of effectivity, that of structural causality) can be entirely summed up in the concept of 'Darstellung', the key epistemological concept of the whole Marxist theory of value, the concept whose object is precisely to designate the mode of presence of the structure in its effects, and therefore to designate structural causality itself...

The structure is not an essence outside the economic phenomena which comes and alters their aspect, forms, and relations and which is effective on them as an absent cause, absent because it is outside them. The absence of the cause in the structure's 'metonymic causality' on its effects is not the fault of the exteriority of the structure with respect to the economic phenomena; on the contrary, it is the very form of the interiority of the structure, as a structure, in its effects. This implies,

> therefore, that the effects are not outside the structure, are not a pre-existing object, element, or space in which the structure arrives to imprint its mark, on the contrary, it implies that the structure is immanent in its effects, a cause immanent in its effects in the Spinozist sense of the term, that the whole existence of the structure consists of its effects, in short, that the structure which is merely a specific combination of its peculiar elements, is nothing outside its effects.[16]

According to Jameson, the targets of Althusser's critique of the concept of 'expressive totality' are not simply Hegel and Hegelian Marxists,[17] but also the more vexed problems of historical periodization. Any worthwhile use of the notion of a historical or cultural period veers in spite of itself towards becoming "a facile totalisation, a seamless web of phenomena, each of which, in its own way, 'expresses' some unified inner truth".[18] Thus, the diversity and complexity of a historical period is reduced to categories such as world-view and period style. However, it needs to be mentioned here that Jameson resists the Althusserian repudiation of the concept of expressive totality and tries to defend its localized employment, with a creative rephrasing of the rather conventional Marxist notion of 'mediation' in terms of what he calls 'transcoding'.

However, beyond the questions of periodization stands the larger, more basic, question regarding the representation of history. According to Jameson, there are two aspects to this: synchronic and diachronic. Firstly, the status of an individual phase whose ingredients are so homogeneously mixed that we see them in terms of a total system or an idealist concept that signifies the whole period. Secondly, we view history as a linear progression of such stages or moments. Jameson believes that the problem of linear sequentiality takes precedence, as individual period formations suggest or project narratives or narrative representations of the historical sequential progression in which they locate themselves and from which they derive their own validity. Jameson, therefore, claims that the most complete articulation of 'expressive causality', or what Althusser calls 'historicism', is a 'vast interpretive allegory' in which history is rewritten in terms of a hidden master narrative, which is the figural content of the sequence of empirical materials.[19] In short, this means that conventional histories are 'stories' that come to mean through allegorical references to an underlying, deeper, more 'fundamental' narrative. It needs to be noted here that Althusser's attack on allegorical master codes also suggests a specific critique of the 'economism' of the vulgar Marxist theory of levels, i.e. the base superstructure model, with its concept of the 'ultimately determining economic instance'.

This is the context in which we should read the famous Althusserian pronouncement, "History is a process without a *telos* or a subject", as a repudiation of master narratives and their categories of narrative closure and of character. Thus, human beings are not the authors or subjects of history, which is decentred and has no motive. This anti-teleological principle of history can be seen as based on Lacan's notion of the 'real' as that which 'resists symbolization absolutely', and so Spinoza's idea of the 'absent cause'. Jameson claims that this sweeping negativity of the Althusserian formulation does not mean that history as a 'referent'[20] does not exist. Instead, he forwards a revised proposition: history is *not* a text, nor a narrative, master or otherwise, but as an absent cause, it is not accessible to us except in textual forms. And, therefore, 'our approach to it and to the 'real' itself necessarily passes through its prior textualization, its narrativization in the political unconscious'.[21]

Such structuralist reinvention of history depends on the complete separation of the conceptual terrain from the real. Thus, for Althusser, the problem of the concept of history is a question of models, and not of realities. He points out that both diachrony and synchrony are conceptual categories and that it is 'lived' history, i.e. the experience of the individual, and 'objective' history, i.e. the unfolding of collective lives, that are the unknowable. Therefore, diachrony, as a mode of thought, according to Althusser, is 'a time of time, a complex time that one cannot read in the continuity of the time of life or of clocks, but that one must construct out of the specific structures of production itself'.[22] This also holds for the concept of synchrony which Althusser sees as an abstraction from the 'richness of the contemporary', of a complex 'structure in dominance'.

Thus, the Althusserian historiographical formulation seeks to repudiate both the empiricist as well as the idealist conceptions of history, which are seen in an assimilated form as two dialectical opposites:

> Here we are at the very antipodes of visible empirical history, where the time of all histories is the simple time of continuity, and where the 'contents' are simply the empty shape of the events which take place in it, which the historian then attempts to order with various editing techniques in order to 'periodize' this continuity. Instead of these categories of the continuous and discontinuous, which make up the flat mystery of ordinary history, we have to deal with infinitely more complex categories, specific to each type of history, where there intervene new logical forms, where to be sure the Hegelian schemes, which are but the sublimation of the categories of the 'logic of movement and time', have nothing but a highly approximate value... for if we take these Hegelian categories for adequate ones, their use would then become theoretically absurd...[23]

In this context, it is important to come back to the Marxist, infrastructure-superstructure paradigm and to look at the ways in which Althusser's theory of structural causality transforms it. Traditional Marxism envisaged – or, in the absence of rigorous conceptualization, perpetuated the impression – that the 'ultimately determining instance' or the mode of production as the narrowly economic level 'determines' the other levels of the manifold social system. In contrast, we notice that the

Althusserian conception of the mode of production identifies itself with the structure as a whole. For Althusser, the narrowly economic, i.e. the forces and the relations of production, the labour processes, and the technical developments, however privileged, do not constitute the mode of production as a whole. It is the larger category of the mode of production that assigns this narrowly 'economic' level its particular role and function, as it does all the others. Thus, in this 'structuralist' Marxist framework, only one kind of structure is posited, and that is the mode of production or the 'synchronic system of social relations as a whole'. In this sense, the 'structure' is an absent cause, as it is nowhere empirically present as an element, is not a part of a whole or one of the levels, but rather the entire system of *relationships* among those levels.[24] Thus, the many levels of the social system are seen to be 'semi-autonomous'. However, it needs to be clarified that this concept of 'semi-autonomy' needs to *relate* as much as it separates. Hence, we can observe that the Althusserian structure, like all Marxisms, necessarily insists on the inter-relatedness of all elements in a social formation. However, it relates them by way of their structural *difference* and distance from one another, rather than by their ultimate identity.[25]

Hence, for Althusser, reality is irreducibly complex and diverse, subject to multiple causations, i.e. 'overdetermined'. In his structuralist framework, historical events are seen as causally 'overdetermined' in the Freudian sense, forming processes of 'displacement' – in terms of the shift from one structure to another – and 'condensation' – when in a radical moment, all the hitherto separate parts of the historical structure become profoundly politicized and identified with each other – and where political upheaval itself is seen as something like the *Darstellung* or representation of those deeper contradictions in the infrastructure which thus ultimately 'express themselves'.[26]

However, it is the superstructure that becomes a terrain of politics in Althusser through the reinsertion of the opposition of infrastructure and superstructure into the mental sphere, i.e. within the superstructure itself. If philosophical positions are systematic variations of an available model or paradigm, then it is vital to chart the conceptual boundaries of that model. This then constitutes a kind of 'bedrock of thought', of a 'theoretical praxis', where it functions as a type of infrastructure for the history of ideas. Althusser names such ideational infrastructure as the *problematique,* or problem-complex. This 'determines' the thinking done in it, as it serves as an absolute limit on thought. This is 'the 'cloture', or conceptual ceiling, inherent in a paradigm that governs the thinking of a given generation'.[27] This implies that the given generation and its historical moment are located within such *problematique,* and genuine historical change would be seen as a sudden replacement of the older problematics by a new one. Consequently, it is through the mediation of the problematic and its epistemological breaks that the realm of the superstructure accesses the momentous changes taking place outside it, in the sphere of 'real history'. Though the shifts within the 'problematic' might not be readily visible, what is accessible to the theoretician is the relationship of the individual philosophic position to the problem-complex on which it is based.[28] Thus, one of the seminal contributions of this structuralist theory of paradigms is that it has brought together the disciplines of philosophy and the history of ideas, in the sense that it has built a systematic, philosophic basis for the methodology of the history of ideas. It can no longer be imagined as an enquiry into trends and comparisons between ideas; instead, it has to be seen as a rigorous mode of research into the necessary system behind ideas.

Hence, it should be understood that the Althusserian formulation reverses the terms of the older materialist epistemology, in which reality is 'outside the mind' and truth a kind of approximation with reality that is rather difficult to verify. According to Althusser, both ideology and genuine philosophical investigation, which he calls the 'theoretical praxis', are activities that begin and end in the mental sphere. Ironically, materialism is sought to be preserved by an insistence on the essentially idealistic nature of all thought. Thus, while ideology passes itself off as reality, theory recognizes its own ideational nature. On another level, ideology can be viewed as the grillwork of form, convention, and belief that orders our actions, while theory is seen as a conscious production of knowledge. Therefore, for Althusser, theory is a kind of production that works with tangible objects which have already been produced, i.e. the earlier theories, and transforms them into new objects. In his formulation, ideology or inadequate conceptualization (which he calls Generality I) is transformed into precise scientific knowledge (Generality III), by the operation of the theoretical praxis (Generality II).[29]

According to Althusser, the relationship between ideational production and material reality could be understood on two levels. The first, on the level of thinking, is that of the *problematique*, an intermediary, hierarchical structure between thought and reality. However, where the level of the thinker is concerned, only the distinction between the theoretical praxis and the political praxis appears to provide a possibility of acting on a real, even though indirectly knowable, world. As Jameson puts it, since for Althusser, real historical time is only indirectly accessible, action for him is a kind of blindfolded operation, a manipulation at a distance, where we can watch our performance only indirectly, as though in a mirror, reading it back from the various readjustments of consciousness, which result from the changes in the external world.[30]

Our account of structuralist historiography would remain radically incomplete if we do not take stock of the early writings of Foucault. In what has been designated as his 'archaeological' phase, Foucault wrote three important texts that seem at first glance to be works of history. These books are *Madness and Civilization: A History of Insanity in the Age of Reason* (1961), *Birth of the Clinic: An Archaeology of Medical Perception*

(1963), and *The Order of Things: An Archaeology of the Human Sciences* (1966). However, their task is not to redescribe historical events, but to bring to life underlying structures of thought and in that sense, they are enquiries into discourse formation. The three texts deal with the discourses of psychiatry, medicine, and the human sciences, respectively, as also the manners in which authoritative discourses comprehended, categorized, and disseminated such nebulous entities as 'sanity', 'health', and 'knowledge' at different phases in the history of Western culture. These complex formulations seek to explain how the distinctions between madness and sanity, sickness and health, and truth and error were always a function of the modality of discourse prevailing in centres of social power at different periods. In Foucault's view, this modality was less a product of autonomous exchange between theory and practice than a product of an endless interaction between desire and power.[31] Thus, rather than revealing the daily lifestyle of a community, as is done by traditional archaeologists, Foucault, as archaeologist, aimed to reveal a people's knowledge style, unearthing the guiding principles and assumptions that operate prior to any assertions about the knowledge of facts.[32] In *The Order of Things*, Foucault characterized his idea of 'archaeology' as follows:

> Quite obviously, such an analysis does not belong to the history of ideas or of science: It is rather an inquiry whose aim is to rediscover on what basis knowledge and theory become possible; within what space of order knowledge was constituted; on the basis of what historical a priori, and in the element of what positivity, ideas could appear, sciences be established, experience be reflected in philosophies, rationalities be formed, only perhaps, to dissolve and vanish soon afterwards. I am not concerned, therefore, to describe the progress of knowledge towards an objectivity in which today's science can finally be recognized; what I am attempting to bring to light is the epistemological field, the *episteme* in which knowledge,

> envisaged apart from all criteria having reference to its rational value or to its objective forms, grounds its positivity and thereby manifests a history which is not that of its growing perfection, but rather that of its conditions of possibility; in this account, what should appear are those configurations within the *space* of knowledge which have given rise to the diverse forms of empirical science. Such an enterprise is not so much a history, in the traditional meaning of that word, as an 'archaeology'.[33]

Here, we notice that history is about its very own conditions of possibility, while the historical a priori becomes the epistemological field, the discursive bedrock that determines all knowledge. Thus, Jameson sees Foucault's work as symptomatic of the process in which 'history' becomes a form of mind among many others.[34] The critical concept central to Foucault's analyses, especially in *The Order of Things*, is that of representation, i.e. a conception of the relationship of idea to object or word to thing, in which the former stands as a mimesis of the latter. Foucault's purpose is to demonstrate the mutations and crises of these relationships:

> ....analysis has been able to show the coherence which existed, throughout the classical age (by this is meant the 17th and 18th centuries), between the theory of representation and the theories of language... It is this configuration that, from the 19th century onward, changes entirely; the theory of representation disappears as the universal foundation for all possible orders.... a profound historicity penetrates to the very heart of things... imposes upon them forms of order implied by the continuity of time... and, above all, language loses its privileged position and becomes, in its turn, a historical form coherent with the density of its own past... man enters in his turn... the field of Western knowledge... From this are born all the chimeras of new humanisms... It is comforting... to think that man is but a recent invention, a figure not yet two centuries old, a simple fold in our knowledge, and that he will disappear again as soon as that knowledge has discovered a new form.[35]

Jameson attempts to analyse this new theory of history by using the historical life of 'language' as a guiding thread: from the Renaissance – where the world is seen through scripture, text, hieroglyph – through the classical period – where grammar and logic dominated – to the modern times – where historical linguistics dominates. Thus, we find that history is marked by a gradual effacement of discourse, which now with the emergence of structuralism, appears to be on the verge of a return to the notion of the pre-eminence of language over history as well as subjectivity. Therefore, Jameson sees in Foucault a reverse teleology and an extreme version of the idea of historical mutation as a radical shift from one internally coherent synchronic moment to the other.[36] It is quite obvious by now that this was a rather harsh judgement[37] of what can be seen in part as an application of the Althusserian *problematique* to unusual areas of historical enquiry, and in part as an advancement over the Althusserian conception of structural totality.

Thus, Jameson argues that structuralism can be best understood as a form of philosophical formalism that has attempted to assimilate within it the two methods of historical materialism and psychoanalytic hermeneutics.[38] However, in the process, it has claimed to dissolve the subject into sheer relationality. This problematic anti-humanist assertion does not, according to Jameson, constitute a liberation from bourgeois subjectivism, but instead structures a 'prison-house' of the symbolic order.[39]

Notes

1. Jean Piaget, *Structuralism*, C. Maschler, Routledge and Kegan Paul, London, 1971. p. 120.
2. Though this paper is not primarily concerned with hermeneutics, it recognizes its importance for the study of history.

3. The structuralisms in question are filtered through Fredric Jameson's supply critique for two reasons. Firstly, the disciplinary location of the critique is more commensurate to my training, and secondly, this, we hope, would arrest the impression that the structuralist theoretical insights are immutable formulae.
4. Piaget uses the expression *'wholeness'*. Piaget, op. cit., p. 6.
5. Ibid., pp. 3-16.
6. Ibid., p. 109.
7. Maurice Godelier, *Perspectives in Marxist Anthropology*, 1977, p. 45; cited from Tom Bottomore et al., (ed.), *A Dictionary of Marxist Thought*, Blackwell Reference, 1983, p. 471.
8. Transcended in the sense of *aufgehebt*, i.e. sublated.
9. Claude Levi-Strauss, *The Savage Mind*, University of Chicago Press, Chicago, 1967, p. 262; cited from Piaget, op. cit., p. 108.
10. Piaget, op. cit., p. 111.
11. Jameson translates this as custom, the original French word being *pratiques.*
12. Levi-Strauss, op. cit., p. 130; cited from Piaget, op. cit., p. 111.
13. Fredric Jameson, *The Prison-House of Language: A Critical Account of Structuralism and Russian Formalism,* Princeton University Press, Princeton, 1972, p. 102.
14. Fredric Jameson, *The Political Unconscious: Narrative as a Socially Symbolic Act*, Routledge, London, 1983, p. xii.
15. Bottomore et al. (ed.) *A Dictionary of Marxist Thought,* pp. 15-16.
16. Louis Althusser et al., *Reading Capital*, (tr.) Ben Brewster, New Left Books, London, 1970, pp. 186-89; cited from Jameson, *The Political Unconscious.*, pp. 8-9.
17. By Hegelian Marxists, we actually mean the Sartrean concept of totalisation and Lukacs's theory of totality.
18. Jameson, *The Political Unconscious,* p. 12.
19. Ibid., p. 13.
20. By which is meant the context, the ground, or the reference to an external reality.
21. Jameson, *The Political Unconscious*, p. 20.
22. Louis Althusser et al., op. cit., pp. 125-26; cited from Jameson, *The Prison-House of Language*, p. 189.
23. Ibid., p. 129; cited from Jameson, ibid., pp. 189-90.
24. Jameson, *The Political Unconscious*, p. 21.

25. Ibid., pp. 25-26.
26. Jameson, *The Prison-House of Language*, p. 121.
27. Ibid., p. 135.
28. Jameson claims that this labour of locating the model behind the idea is what Derrida calls 'deconstruction', Jameson, ibid., p. 136.
29. Ibid., p. 108.
30. Ibid., p. 108.
31. Hayden White, 'Michel Foucault', in *Structuralism and Since: From Levi-Strauss to Derrida,* John Sturrock (ed.), Oxford University Press, Oxford, 1979, pp.90-91.
32. Robert Wicks, 'Michel Foucault', in *The Blackwell Guide to Continental Philosophy*, Robert Solomon and David Sherman (eds.), Blackwell, Oxford, 2003, p. 251.
33. Michel Foucault, *The Order of Things: An Archaeology of the Human Sciences,* Vintage Books, New York, 1994, pp. xxi-xxii.
34. Jameson, *The Prison-House of Language*, p. 191.
35. Foucault, op. cit., p. xxiii. Translation amended with the help of the quotation cited in Jameson, ibid., pp. 191-92.
36. Ibid., pp. 193-94.
37. It should be noted that Jameson's discussion of Foucault in *The Prison-House of Language* (published in 1972) could be one of the earliest assessments of Foucault's work in the Anglophone world.
38. Jameson, op. cit., p. 195.
39. Ibid., pp. 139-40.

7

History through the Gender Lens

Maithreyi Krishnaraj

The process of women becoming conscious of their place in history, and their relation to history, begins with their engagement with feminism. Feminism discovered that what we consider as history and who gets to write history, who are the subjects of history, are all subject to a 'gender' bias. It is men who get to write history; they decide who is important, and if they write about women, it is through men's eyes. Feminism's engagement with history led to three kinds of endeavours: (1) identifying the absence of women and realizing how most of human history is about men, (2) identifying the biases in the representation of women – if and when women do get included, and (3) writing their own history.

Since history is about the past, and past records happen to be scanty on women, if women have to rewrite history, a new historiography is needed. They have to struggle for sources beyond men's records, move beyond conventional methodologies and beyond existing frameworks. This is not easy. To quote Bourdieu (1990):

> The dominant agents appear distinguished because, being so born into a position that is distinguished positively, their habitus, their socially constituted nature is immediately adjusted

> to the immanent demands of the game and they can thus assert their difference without needing to want to, that is with the unselfconsciousness that is the mark of natural distinction.

Women have to strive for distinction, whereas men already possess distinction. Feminist historiography has to proceed to demonstrate that there is a 'gendering' process which is unnatural. Men write history because they have the power and they control the public realm. History is defined as what happens in the 'public realm'. The rewriting of history by those who were excluded from the public realm can be achieved by challenging this invidious distinction that fragments human lives. This is more true of women than of the subaltern.

What feminist historians have done is to begin with existing frameworks, critique them, and refine them. Much of their efforts involve re-interpretations as well as looking for hidden clues in existing sources. This new historiography runs in parallel tracks: to assert that women's experiences are different because they are women, and to wish simultaneously to incorporate women into a common human history. The assumption in the first case is that history will always be gendered, that there will be men's history and women's history; in the second case, that there is a common humanity which, once de-gendered, will be human history. Feminist historians thus tread an ambiguous path. In challenging the universalist grand narratives that inscribe women in them, and replacing them with specific and differential knowledge, a tension inevitably results, where the outcome will be several histories – pick your choice.

Feminist history writing began as an unexplored territory, lacking precedents and lacking readily available source material. In a way, this was advantageous. They could innovate and experiment and, hence, they toyed with different tools and less accepted sources like diaries and oral testimonies. In approaching history, the initial effort was to put women into history by documenting their contribution to human civilization. The second was to detect how this omission happened by undertaking studies in several fields such as anthropology, sociology, history 'proper', economics, politics, and a whole range of explorations. For example, a crop of books came up in the 1960s: *Towards an Anthropology of Women* (Reiter, 1982). There were books tracing the history of psychology, science, sociology, politics, literature, and so on. Developing a feminist historiography emerged as the culmination of feminist theory, exploring various disciplines to evolve an interdisciplinary thrust.

Today, history is not about wars, empires, conquests, dynasties, and leaders, but about society, social changes, and different actors in society. It is primarily about civilizations, their art, culture, philosophies, and religion. Thus, history is a part of women's studies, which inevitably drew from multiple disciplines. We do not as yet have a comprehensive history of civilization pertaining to women, while there are many that deal with general civilizational progress. Civilizational history requires drawing from many sources: art, archaeology, technology, science, politics, literature, and so on. Written documents in the form of archives provide little help. Of all the disciplines, anthropology provided the richest material. One could reasonably ascertain how women lived in the past. Anthropological writings showed how women have been active in all social spheres from the earliest times. Agriculture and crafts like basketry are women's innovations. When communities are described, mainstream writings talk of hunter-gatherer, pastoral, or agricultural communities without mention of who did what. Historically, women provided the bulk of food and continue to do so even today. Women produce 70 per cent of the food in the world, according to the International Labour Organization and the Food and Agricultural Organization, both part of the United Nations. Yet, history mentions Man the Hunter as the architect of human civilization. A recent study of forest societies in Asia talks of women who even undertook big game hunting in India

(Kelkar and Nathan, 2003). In the beginning, geographers were not involved in looking at gender. There is now not only an international feminist geography journal but one of our foremost geographers, Saraswati Raju, is currently working on how geography affects patriarchy to answer why it is that the South of India is less gender asymmetric than the North. Turning to the arts, women are said to be more involved in crafts and, therefore, do not qualify as Artists with a big A. Who defines what art is and the boundary between art and craft? This is a question of the power to define what is commendable and what is not. There is today a lot of effort by women to bring to light women's contribution to the arts in the form of quilt making, weaving, mat weaving, ceramics, and folk decorative art, such as floor designs or wall designs. A similar effort was made for the performing arts. Sparrow, a women's organization in Mumbai, documents and collects such records to create a new women's history.

These parallel practices intend to create a parallel social space within the domains of existing social life, constantly contesting the dominance by men in order to finally replace current practices with new ones, not just to get immediate relief, but with the underlying intent of subverting the system that perpetuates male dominance. Both the need for an identity which negates the imposed one as well as the character of the emerging forms are influenced by the specific history of domination and dispossession. The questioning and reconstructing of identities have to take place in the context of their hegemonic history. The task is more than a simple negation and simple inversion. It results in creating new mythologies to escape oppression past and present. Dalit history is full of this fallacy. Nanda cautions us against this kind of approach, which valorises uncritically traditional practices (Nanda, 1995, 1996).

A basic premise in writing women's history is that patriarchy as a system of male domination evolved to produce female subordination. Feminist historians like Gerda Lerner have tried to give a historical account of the creation of patriarchy (Learner, 1986). While inter-disciplinarity was inevitable because gender enters into every aspect of our lives, conceptual problems plague our efforts to introduce gender. What exactly is gender? Gender is a relational concept in which a woman and a man stand in a certain relation to each other. It is also identity. One's consciousness is that of a woman or man. It is also a particular ideology using symbolic tools. I did a simple exercise in one training programme. Each woman was asked to write five lines about herself. Every one of them began by saying, "I am a woman." No one said, "I am Gita, or Rashida, or Christine."

Do women form one category? In a society divided by class, caste, and race, which betray hierarchies of power, do all women face the same oppression? Is all oppression and subordination only by men on women? These questions still demand satisfying answers and the theory of patriarchy soon ran into trouble as a framework for women's history, that is women's history as the history of women under patriarchy, and as the history of the decline of matriarchy (Reed, 1975; Bachofen, 1967).

History occurs over time and space. The course of history is delineated in 'periods'. Does Hobsbawm's monumental works, *The Age of Revolution, The Age of the Empire, The Age of Capital, and The Age of Uncertainty,* have parallels in feminist history? (Rupa reprint, 1992) *The Underside of History* by Elise Boulding (1976) adopts the historical materialism approach. Using anthropological data and the literature on antiquity about Stone Age, Palaeolithic Agro Village Sites of West Asia and the Mediterranean, she traces the history of women's lives as the unreported underlife. The societal types she follows as the evolutionary path are band and tribal, pre-urban, city based states, centralized bureaucratic empire, and modern industrialized states. Beginning with activities that were dominant in each period, she tries to retrieve the activity of women – hunting, gathering, settled agriculture, trading, city-states, empires ancient, mediaeval, modern, etc. The history runs from 50,000 BC to the 20th century. The book contrasts the predominantly human welfare orientation of women's activities in all social classes and the predominantly conquest and domination orientation of male activities. That contrast essentially remains unchanged, even when city life becomes the focal point of one's life. Boulding explores the underlife structures for women and how these structures shaped women's life and behaviour. There is an overlife that corresponds to the underlife, which consists of overtly articulated roles. Women may keep a public stance and yet manage to express resistance. The underlife is not clandestine, it has something to do with spatial differentiation, the public-private distinction, or the visible invisible locations.

In the Indian context, historical research and writing on women took conventional paths, dividing periods into ancient, mediaeval, and modern. To this day, we still follow this periodisation, regardless of whether they are relevant or not for women. Alternatively, there is an attempt to see how women fared under different cultures or religious orders – women under Buddhism, under Jainism, under Hinduism, under Christianity, under Islam, and so on. This is done by reading the scriptural texts to see what they say about women what injunctions, what prejudices, what liberties, or rights are given under each order (Bhattacharjee, 1990, 1996). The incidental nature of references to women in 'regular' history pertained only to elite women or extraordinary women. They talked of queens who wielded power or of exceptional women like warrior women or saint women. Before independence, the nationalist upsurge provoked eulogistic tomes on 'Great Women of India', which selected extraordinary women, partly historical, partly mythological. These were attempts to set the record straight regarding the status of women in India to counter the castigation of Hindu society by the colonizers. Altekar's book is a standing testimony to this genre (Altekar, 1962).

The feminists in independent India expose the male bias in ancient India through the analysis of Brahminical scriptures like Bhattacharjee, Roy, and Chakravarty. There are others like the critiques of Hindu society by Pandita Rama Bai and Tarabai Shinde. Indian feminists today resurrect models from ancient India, but reinterpret them as rebels, instead of portraying them as iconic devotees of patriarchal values (Manushi, 1989). Alongside there is also a spate of studies on postcolonial India as well as those that talk of reconstructing patriarchy by the colonizers and the nationalists. This literature is particularly abundant in Bengali writing. Much of this kind of history writing had very limited parameters and did not base their analysis on the totality of the social formation that would include the economic, social, cultural, and political. It was only Uma Chakravarty, Kumkum Roy, and Kumkum Sangari who set about doing this (see the list of books appended at the end of this essay.) While Chakravarty and Roy confine themselves to scriptural texts, Sangari broke free of this textual immanence by exploring other sources, which are amorphous in form like prescriptive manuals, school textbooks, proceedings of learned societies, religious organizations, pamphlets, songs, caste associations, essays, missionary treatises, administrative documents, court proceedings, etc. (Sangari, 1999). Today, there are histories of regions, of institutions, of women's education, and of women's struggles (see list of books at the end).

Adequately theorized history writing comes from the Marxists. They had an explanation that covered the social formation and its changes over time, what were the engines of change, and how they affected the relations among different social actors. It was the history of class struggle and women's subordination was subsumed under the class. Socialist feminists carried forward the insights and methodology of Marxist history, but contested this subsumption. Women as women had a separate oppression apart from those belonging to their class. Marxist history is grounded in historical materialism, which advances the following propositions. In the social production of life, men enter into definite relations of production like that between the feudal lord and the serf, and the capitalist and the worker. These relations are indispensable and independent of their will, and correspond to that stage of development of material forces like technology. The sum total of these relations of production constitutes, the economic structure of society, which is the foundation on which culture, consciousness, and ideology emerge. Engels' classic text on the subjugation of women uses this framework to write the history of women's subordination (Engels, reprint, 1978). As long as women's labour was critical to the economy and men and women performed their roles equally, women had no problem and they were valued. It was the rise of domesticity for women and men's work in production for the market, with factory production displacing household production, that resulted in loss of visibility to women's contribution and, hence, its undervaluation. Up until the 18th century, 90 per cent of all production was in the household. Even today, women's household production is substantial in the Third World, but with the rise of market production, it is invisible. The solution offered by the Marxists was that women must move to social production. Other Marxist feminists pointed to Engles' assumptions that domestic labour did not produce anything except consumption and, therefore, did not enter into 'relations of production', whereas it contributed to the capital by getting the man-worker cheap in as much as it did not need to pay enough for his daily upkeep, which was taken care of by women at home doing it free. For one wage, the capitalist got two workers. Many Marxist women in India, too, give overwhelming importance to women's labour and women's subordination due to sexual division of labour.

A great deal of empirical work has shown that however much women participate in paid labour, it does not necessarily lessen subordination because women face discrimination at the workplace, too. The role of ideology is important here and not only material forces. The subordination of women at home is transferred to the marketplace. It lays down what work women can do, what rewards they can get. The definition of women as secondary earners means that women can be fired any time. A great deal of work today in India and elsewhere is on women's work. Labour history dominates women's history. It was the socialist feminists who pointed out the role of ideology. They emphasized that ideology was not a mere superstructure to the economic base. It enjoyed an autonomy of its own. Women undertaking market work in the public sphere does not exonerate them from patriarchal relations. The socialist feminists' signal contribution was to draw attention to the relations of reproduction: reproducing the human being through childbirth, reproducing the human being through nourishment and care, and reproducing the social structure itself. In all three aspects, sexuality and its control play a critical role. Women do not have much say in whether they want a child, son or daughter; they do not have much freedom in sexual relations. They have to abide by existing rules of sexual conduct with its manifold taboos regarding acceptable conduct for women. Often, men asserting their virility demand children while childbearing is a huge stress for women. This has led to new explorations on the history of sexual relations (Barrett, 1980, 1992).

Basically, the structural approach was propounded by feminist theories regarding patriarchy. Most of women's history today falls into this genre, where patriarchy is accepted as a 'system' outside individual actions. The contribution of women in the Third World lies in using patriarchy, not as one universal system, but as something that is specific to each society. They showed that patriarchy was not a universal, seamless, integrated phenomenon. The parameters of patriarchy operated radically differently in different societies (Krishnaraj, 1999, 2000). What Western feminists proposed was true only of the white middle class in a capitalist society. The theory excluded considerations of race and class. This was the beginning of the change in the approach to history. The challenge lay in rejecting the grand narrative of patriarchy because it came in conflict with local knowledge and specific semiotic systems that do not transcend the geo-historical, linguistic realities of the culture concerned. For example, the problem of dowry is specific to South Asia. Another big difference was that Third World societies did not have the same kind of nuclear families, but had extended families with strong kinship rules. Age and kinship installed another hierarchy to gender hierarchy. Female networks and female culture gave space to women in these societies muting the severity of the patriarchal practices.

Much effort went into showing how women in the Third World, through history, mounted resistances to male dominance. The history of patriarchy now took the form of challenges to patriarchy under new economic and sociopolitical contexts and how patriarchy gets reconstituted. Admittedly, gender is not a voluntarily disposable individual characteristic. One can change one's class by becoming wealthy. Fundamentally, all feminism, no matter of what category, addresses the extraction and transfer of benefits from women to men on a global scale.

The strength of feminism lay in experimentation with different methodologies, avoiding the aping of the unitary categories of the mainstream philosophy of history. They veered away from one position, one truth for all women. Patriarchy has graduated into an adjectival phase, where we talk of different kinds of patriarchies (Chakravarty and Sangari, 2004, 1995). There followed a long period of critique of positivism and structural functionalism. Positivism conceives of society as composed of discrete autonomous individuals who are self-regulating. Changes in these discrete compartments are also autonomous events. The departure from positivism came in trying to work out how different social movements can retain their specificity and yet link them to other social realities. This was a dilemma because if each group's experience was different, how does one evolve resistance or bring about change?

'Standpoint' theorist Sandra Harding believed that reading of events and the reading of history must come from women's experience. This can give the point of view of the oppressed. It is not as simple as it sounds. Can we take women's experience as self-evident? The nature of the experience has a constructed quality. Women's experience simply exists. A standpoint can emerge only after critical reflection. Women's experience needs to be interrogated from a vantage point that is not always available to the local culture and tradition. An Indian woman's experience gets interpreted differently once it is exposed to notions of women's liberation. For women's experiences to be transformed into a feminist standpoint, the liberatory possibilities of their lives have to be amplified through the critical perspective that feminist struggles provide. A feminist standpoint is what orders and interprets women's experiences, but it cannot be reduced to the experiences themselves.

In the course of doing personal interviews for a project on working class women, we found that the subjects went into all kinds of irrelevant accounts, which made it difficult for us to decide what was relevant to understanding women's subordination. The standpoint theory has been widely used in oral history. I am reminded of a seminar in Thiruvananthapuram. Selected women narrated their experience of three generations of women in their families, which was subsequently published. Some of the women who narrated their experiences were known to me personally and their account of their lives departed fundamentally from the actual events of which I was aware. For example, the husband was accused of all kinds of misdeeds, including philandering, while the accounts of many affairs the woman had herself had, were suppressed. Some time ago, a notable feminist, who hails from an extremely wealthy and privileged family, wrote a newspaper account of how she had struggled to rise from a working class background. Here is a kind of feminist consciousness that reinterprets experiences to suit the image of the valiant victim surmounting odds. I am wary of the excessive reliance placed nowadays by feminist historians on so-called oral history. When I raised this question, I was told that what mattered was the woman's point of view –

it was not the authenticity of events that mattered! Chronologically, first comes experience, then comes feminism; standpoint is the end result. Standpoint theorists hardly tell us what there is in women's lives that leads to a feminist understanding of the female experience in the past. The moot question is what aspects of women's individual and collective lives are epistemologically relevant for women. Their methodology has a circular logic. Gender differences explain women's experiences and women's experiences explain gender. It leaves no room for a critique of the existing social order because the idea of legitimate male-female experiences incorporates existing normative definitions. Before making any meaning out of a subject, we have to understand that the subject is already constituted. Feminism accepts that subjectivities are constructed out of experiences which are made of available knowledge and discourses in a culture. The culture discourses are bound by and operate in a totality of the social institutions and material practices, which are hierarchically organized in existing societies, and thus have to be studied within that social totality which extends beyond the local to the global.

Postmodernists seek inter alia to develop conceptions of social criticism, which do not rely on any philosophical underpinning. Criticism floats free of any universal theoretical ground. Social criticism becomes pragmatic, ad hoc, contextual, and local. There are many discourses of legitimation. They declare as illegitimate large historical stories, and normative theories of justice or social theoretical accounts of macro-structures, which institutionalize inequality. In literature, the effect of postmodernism is apparent where scholars are overly preoccupied with 'representation'. Apart from postmodernism's engagement with the specificity of experience (Dalit, local, subaltern, tribal, etc.), general history writing on women is embedded in large social theories such as those of history, sociology, or psychology.

The much acclaimed interdisciplinary approach also has problems. Each discipline has its conceptual categories. Let us take the example of a history of violence against women. A history student would locate the source in criminal records, coroner's proceedings, police files, and newspaper reports. The enquiry gets confined to reported cases. As we all know, women have an enormous disincentive to report cases of violence.

Another kind of problem lies in the insistence on difference. There are differences between societies and between class, caste, and other categories. There are then multiple subjects and multiple histories. As socially situated subjectivity invalidates pure knowledge of the past, generalized propositions are rejected. We end up reporting specific instances. This happened to A and this happened to B. So? What can we say about history? Are not A and B connected to something larger?

Coming to subaltern history, the postcolonial stance of subaltern history leads to defence of tradition even when these practices are harmful and clearly violate the canons of justice. According to these scholars, who is to say sati is bad? It is the prejudiced Western eye which says it is. In the Indian ethos, sacrifice is a great virtue and women who undertake self-immolation are honoured. It is a cultural value, according to those who reject the Orientalism of the West. Similarly, Ashis Nandy argued that poverty is a term invented by the West. Indian language tradition has only *garibi*, which means vulnerability, helplessness. Poverty, therefore, does not exist in India! Rather a comforting thought if the person saying it is not poor. One can defend Indian practices in the name of them being part of our tradition. This is pretty close to the Hindutva ideology. The subaltern studies hardly care to understand that the paradigm they offer is not just a model of an intellectual exercise, but an expression of social ideologies.

To understand extra-historical influences on the process of choosing paradigms for history writing, we must undertake a broader political, cultural context in which the work of the historian is located. History from below need not glorify different communities, whether poor or tribal or Dalit. In the name of celebrating differences, we cannot ignore things which are wrong according to some universal ethic of right and wrong. Ultimately, one has to apply a universal value, however glorious one wants one's own heritage to be. Recently, a PhD student came to me to discuss her work on the Gandhian philosophy of education. Throughout her essay, she made the claim that modern India has lost her glorious 'traditional values'. I asked her which values? The caste system that kept some as scavengers and treated them with such contempt? Has not the march of democracy in India brought some good values, too, replacing authoritarian values and, for the first time, allowed some power to the lower castes? Is there not a greater effort to bring about equality between men and women? She was uncomfortable with my criticism and went away not wanting to consult a professor who did not endorse her vague generalized notion of a perfect past.

A serious problem in feminist historiography is the problem of agency. Do things only happen to women or do women also make things happen? Are they only objects or are they subjects? There are now attempts to show women were not passive victims. Any rebellious act is held up as proof of resistance. Women in the Bhakti movement are often held up as rebels. What is missed out is that though these women no doubt discarded normal life, they secured sainthood *within accepted parameters*. A woman could renounce husband and family if she took to bhakti. Not if she went to live by herself or sought a profession (Khandelwal, 1997). The devotional path was one possible escape route from the tyranny of family and society. Reading agency into these actions is reading more than is warranted by the historical context. We can use the notion of Bourdieu's *habitus* to understand women's agency as Kalpagam does (Kalpagam, 2000). It is said you imbibe something from the social set-up in which you are placed. You develop a strategy at a conscious level. You develop a common-sense approach to problems you confront. The strategy you select is a kind of agency from your unconscious because you plan and execute only what is possible within the set-up. The agency rooted in your environment is like fish that do not speak about water. This is not conscious resistance. It is virtue made out of necessity. As Bourdieu explains, the setting in which one lives (the *habitus*) produces strategies, which even if not consciously produced out of explicitly formulated goals on the basis of adequate knowledge of objective conditions, do help the person to cope with her present situation. This gives us some clue as to why patriarchy could continue and how and why women put up with it. It could be argued that a kind of adjustment was worked out (bargaining?) within the given set-up to create some space for women. To give such practices an active inventive intention, one can argue that even in an apparently oppressive situation, there is an element of agency. A prisoner refuses to eat. A woman may deny some service to her spouse. A worker may go on strike. There is always a common-sense grasp of what one can do in a given situation. Until recently, grass-roots women's movements were not accepted as 'feminist' by urban feminists because women were fighting for water or land, and not explicitly feminist goals such as eliminating sexual division of labour or challenging sexual control of women. The struggles of these women for bread and butter issues can be taken as steps towards building a feminist thrust. We hear often that women's groups constituted for credit, once they come together, find strength to take up domestic violence issues and alcoholism of men. The agency here may seem to fall short of the challenge of feminism, but could move from the unconscious to the consciously formulated challenge to patriarchy. So the shift today in women's history writing is to shift the focus from women as victims to women as agents.

Apart from recording women's contribution to the history of their societies, women are also involved in 'the history in the making' through individual action as well as collective action. Women's archives are capturing this through biography, autobiography, and through oral testimony. The repository of myths and legends, folk tales, folk art, and folk music belongs to the cultural history of a region or community. These are delved into to shape the meaning of the present, to guide action, to give ideals, through retelling, through re-interpretation. There are now many *Ramayanas*; many versions of Draupadi's story. These informal ways of coping with history writing in the absence of formal records are not given their share in the official record of 'making history'. In every society and time, totalitarian regimes have rewritten history. How much of the 'actual' remains then in one's collective memory? Methods of history writing deal with what sources are used, how they are interpreted. History is ultimately an exercise in sampling.

If history is all about the past, antecedent events, how do we come to terms with its influence in the present, or how does our present colour our past? When gender consciousness becomes universal, how will our history be? Will we still be gendered beings?

Further Readings

Altekar, A.S., *The Position of Women in Hindu Civilization*, Motilal Banarasidas, New Delhi, 1962.

Bachofen, J.J. (tr.), *Myth and Mother Right,* Routledge and Kegan Paul, London, 1967.

Bagchi, Jasodhara, 'Positivism and Nationalism, Womanhood and Crisis in Nationalist Fiction: Bankimchandra's *Anandmath*', in *Economic and Political Weekly,* Vol. 20, No. 43, October 26, 1990.

Barrett, Michele and Anne Philips (ed.), *Destabilizing Theory. Contemporary Feminist Debates,* Polity Press, Cambridge, 1992.

Barrett, Michele, *Women's Oppression Today. Problems in Marxist Feminist Analysis,* New Left Books, London,1980.

Bhattacharjee, Sukumari, "Motherhood in Ancient India," in *Economic and Political Weekly,* October 20-27, 1990.

—, "Demythologizing Early Indian History," *Economic and Political Weekly,* September 28, 1996.

Boulding, Elise, *The Underside of History: A View of Women Through Time*, West View Press, Boulder, Colorado, 1976.

Bourdieu, Pierre, *In other Words: Essays Towards Reflexive Sociology,* Stanford University Press, Stanford, 1990.

Chakravarty, Uma and Kumkum Roy, 'In Search of Our Past: A Review of the Limitations and Possibilities of Historiography of Women in Early India', in *Economic and Political Weekly,* Vol. 23, No. 18, 30 April, 1988.

Chakravarty, Uma, *Reinscribing the Past: Inserting Women into Indian History,* Beam, Mumbai, 1995.

—, *Rewriting History: The Life and Times of Pandita Ramabai,* Kali for Women, New Delhi, 1998.

Chatterjee, Partho, 'Nationalist Resolution of the Women's Question' in Sudesh Vaid and Kumkum Sangari (eds.), *Recasting Women: Essays in Colonial History,* Kali for Women, Delhi, 1989.

Dube, Leena, 'Who Gains from Matriarchy? Men, Women and Change in a Lakshadweep Island', *Sociological Bulletin,* Vol. 42, Nos. 1&2, March-September, 1993.

Engels, Friedrich (Reprint), *The Origin of the Family, Private Property and the State,* International Publishers, New York, 1978.

Harding, Sandra, *The Instability of Analytical Categories of Feminist Theory,* SIGNS, Summer 1986.

Hobsbawm, E.J., (1962, 1975, 1987), *The Age of Revolution, The Age of Capital, The Age of Empire.* Rupa Paperbacks, 1992.

Kalpagam, U., 'Life Experiences, Resistances and Feminist Consciousness', *Indian Journal of Gender Studies,* Vol. 7, Nos. 2, 2000.

Kapur, Ratna, *Feminist Terrains in Legal Domain in India,* Kali for Women, New Delhi, 1996.

Kosambi, Meera, 'Women, Emancipation and Equality: Pandita Ramabai's Contribution to Women's Cause'. *Economic and Political Weekly,* 29 October 1988.

Krishnaraj, Maithreyi, 'Writing Women's History or Writing Women into History?' in Kirit K. Shah (ed.) *History and Gender: Some Explorations,* Rawat Publications, Jaipur, 2005.

Kumar, Radha, *History of Doing: Illustrated Account of Women's Movement in India,* Kali for Women, New Delhi, 1993.

Lerner, Gerda, *The Creation of Patriarchy,* Oxford University Press, London, 1986.

Linda J. Nicholson (ed.), *Feminism and Post Modernism,* Routledge, London, 1990.

Manushi (journal) 'Women Bhakti Poets', Nos. 50, 51, 52, 1989.

Mead, Margaret, *Sex and Temperament in Three Primitive Societies*, San Diego, New York/London, 1950.

Reed, Evelyn, *Women's Evolution from Matriarchal Clan to Patriarchal Family*, Pathfinder Press, New York, 1975.

Reiter, Rayna, *Towards an Anthropology of Women*, Monthly Review Press, New York, 1982.

Roy, D.K., *Women in Peasant Movements, Tebhaga, Naxalite and After*, 1992.

Sangari, Kumkum, 'Politics of Diversity: Religious Communities and Multiple Patriarchies', *Economic and Political Weekly*, 30 December 1995.

—, *Politics of the Possible: Essays on Gender, History Narratives, Colonial English.* Tulika, New Delhi, 1999.

Sen, Illina, *A Space Within Struggles*, Kali for Women, New Delhi, 1990.

Stree Shakti Sanghatna, *We were Making History*, Kali for Women, New Delhi, 1989.

Tharu, Susie (ed.), *Women's Writing in India*, Vol. 2, Oxford University Press, Delhi, 1992.

Thorner, Alice and Maithreyi Krishnaraj, *Ideals, Images and Real Lives: Women in Literature and History*, Orient Longman, Hyderabad, India, 2000.

Vaid, Sudesh and Kumkum Sangari, "Institutions, Beliefs, Ideologies: Widow Immolation in Contemporary Rajasthan", *Economic and Political Weekly*, 27 April 1991.

8

A Survey of the Subaltern Historiography of India

Radhika Seshan

In strictly lexical terms, the word 'subaltern' means a junior officer in the army. It therefore refers to someone who holds an inferior rank in a fairly rigidly constituted hierarchy. Antonio Gramsci, the Italian Marxist (and leader of the communist party), used the word in the latter sense, of someone who is subordinated because of being on the lower or lowest rungs of a social hierarchy. Obviously, the opposite of subordination is dominance, and so, subaltern would then automatically mean one who is dominated because of the nature of subordination. Gramsci went on to say that the "history of subaltern social groups is necessarily fragmented and episodic.... Subaltern groups are always subject to the activity of ruling groups...."[1] History does not take into account such 'fragmentary' activities, and so, the subaltern is not just marginalized, but also invisible.

The Subaltern Studies Project drew much of its inspiration from the ideas of Gramsci. The project was launched in the early 1980s, primarily by Ranajit Guha, who went on to edit its first six volumes. These volumes had various themes which ranged from critiques of elite historiography, attempting to understand peasant belief systems, peasant movements, peasant revolts, Indian nationalism, sectarianism, the colonial construction of communalism, power relations within the community, peasant insurgency, subaltern consciousness and politics, the people's perception of Gandhi, Gandhi's politics, the mentalities of the people, the character of the state, the ecological dimension of peasant protest, tribal protest, patterns of liquor consumption, Western medicine and caste, critique of feminist writings, crime in the context of the nationalist movement, and even a few critiques of subaltern studies. The range is, as is obvious, extremely wide, but what is equally striking is that there are very few papers dealing with the working-class movement.

The later volumes have been edited by Shahid Amin and Partha Chatterjee, or by Shahid Amin and Dipesh Chakrabarty, and all the volumes have been published by the Oxford University Press. They mark a change from the earlier volumes, not just in the editors, but also in content. The essays in these volumes revolve mainly around the nation, the community, the Bengali middle class, forest people, colonial prisons, India's partition and historiography, and Indian religion and language. Almost the entire series is available in paperback editions. In addition, in 1988, Ranajit Guha and Gayatri Chakravorty Spivak edited and published a volume entitled *Selected Subaltern Studies*.

The project marked the effort by a group of conscientious Indian historians to rethink the nature of the approach to the writing of Indian history. Sceptical about the models employed in researching India's past, they embarked on a critique of the way Indian history had been projected until then. They pointed to the element of 'top downwards' that was present in such researches, and argued that this tended to obscure the nature of protest by putting it into 'elite' categories. According to Dipesh Chakrabarty, the starting point of the project was a questioning of 'the category of the 'nation' ', and the 'failure of the 'nation' to come to its own as a fundamental problem of modern Indian history'.[2] This basic idea was further amplified by Guha, who explicitly stated that dominant ideology, designated 'statism' by him, determines what is 'historic' and what is not. So, "statism...thematizes and evaluates the past."[3] Not surprisingly, the project focussed itself on what has been termed the 'modern' period of Indian history, i.e. colonialism, the anti-colonial struggles, the movement for independence, etc. The idea was to try and narrate the history of those who had until then been ignored by history – the peasants, tribals, outcastes, etc. However, as most of this is also loosely linked with the idea of the 'advent of the Europeans', there are also a few articles on the pre-colonial period, specifically, those of Gautam Bhadra on peasant revolts in the late Mughal period. The focus is, in other words, mainly on the 19th and 20th centuries, with occasional forays into the 18th century also.

In the first volume, Guha declared that the 'historiography of Indian nationalism' had been dominated by elitism. Elitism in this context generally referred to the Indian national leadership, and the national leaders' consciousness of nationhood. The elites were, however, also collaborators in colonialism. Thus, elitist writings reflected and sustained an elite national consciousness, which carried within it some of the features of colonialism itself. Elitism was of two kinds, 'colonialist' (which he equated with the Cambridge school of historiography) and 'bourgeois-nationalist'[4] (the nationalist school). The creation of the Indian nation was, in this historiography, discussed as though it were a purely elite achievement. Depending on the school of historiography, credit for creating the nation was given either to the British colonial rulers and administrators (in the Cambridge school), or to the Indian elite personalities (nationalist school). Indian nationalism was thus seen as a manifestation of the challenge/response paradigm. Guha argued that while such historiography was undoubtedly useful, especially for increasing the understanding of the "structure of the colonial state, the operation of its various organs in certain historical circumstances, the nature of the alignment of classes which sustained it, some aspects of the ideology of the elite as the dominant ideology of the period",[5] it was, nevertheless, limited. Such writing was unable to explain "the contribution made by people *on their own,* that is, *independent of the elite*".[6] In other words, the existing historiography failed to "acknowledge the subaltern as the maker of his own destiny".[7]

The Subaltern Studies Project started essentially as an attempt to study those groups who were involved in the struggle for freedom, but at different levels and in different ways. It seeks to analyse the Indian national movement in a manner which places the subaltern at the centre, i.e. it begins with the premise that the subaltern acts, and is not merely acted upon. It is fundamentally different from a populist exercise, which tends to treat 'the people' as an undifferentiated category. It can thus be seen as an attempt to retrieve some of the history of the marginalized, so as to recover the 'small voices of history'.

How this was to be done was a question that occupied many of the scholars. A major problem with marginalized groups is that they are often non-literate, and so labelled 'traditional'. Such societies have a history, of course, but this history is 'different', it is variously categorized as myth or memory, and in the post-Enlightenment world, history (as a discipline) had no place for such imprecise practices.[8] It was precisely this aspect that the subaltern groups homed in on. It was pointed out that the moment when the official records 'noted' the groups, and that when the groups 'inscribed' themselves, was not the same. The lapse constituted memory. It was, therefore, pointed out that subaltern histories were "constructed within a particular kind of historical memory, one that remembers history itself as a violation, an imperious code that accompanied the civilizing process that the European Enlightenment inaugurated in the 18th century as a world historical task. This memory does not have the character of nostalgia, for it bespeaks a pain that is in no sense historical in our part of the world."[9]

It is for this reason that many of the essays contained in the volumes revolve around the theme of 'consciousness', and of "subaltern consciousness as emergent collective consciousness".[10] The perspective expressed in the various studies undoubtedly had much in common with the history-from-below approach of some British Marxists, notably E.P. Thompson and Eric Hobsbawm. However, those involved in the project insist that 'similar' does not mean 'same', and there are definitely some differences. Subaltern historiography primarily involves a critique of the nation form, and so, an attempt to study and interrogate the relationship between power and knowledge. The studies make an attempt to redefine the category called 'the political', so as to try and write 'the politics of the people'.

In contrast to conventional Marxist approaches, the subalterns, at least in the early years, studied peasant movements rather than the workers' movements alone. Conventional Marxist historiography had tended to look at peasant revolts as manifestations of a 'backward' consciousness because they were generally organized along lines of kinship and/or religion. Subaltern historiography, in contrast, argued that such consciousness reflected the Gramscian notion of spontaneity, which was not the result of education, but of 'common sense' and 'instinct', which, embedded as they were in practice, had a reality which could not be defined in empiricist terms alone. Thus, peasant consciousness, as seen in peasant movements, far from being backward, actually reflected the peasants' engagement with modernity, for they represented a new arena of political activity in which mobilization took place through powerful symbols. The peasants, living within the colonial world, were part of a colonial modernity. Peasant consciousness was therefore of that modernity, even if the mobilization was around older, traditional symbols. They could by no means be called backward. Peasant revolts might use the familiar symbols of revolt, but the focus of revolt was colonialism. They were thus part of the struggle against colonialism as a whole. Colonial India saw a large number of peasant revolts, spread across diverse regions, and groups around even more diverse symbols. The Subaltern school argued that such revolts had a commonality – that of a subaltern spontaneity and consciousness. Peasant revolts challenged authority by inverting the symbols of that authority, and by trying to destroy such symbols. Violence was a characteristic of peasant revolts, but this was a reflection of their understanding of the nature of their domination, and thus their reaction to it. Religion was undoubtedly a key factor in such revolts, but religion per se was not the prime focus. Peasant revolts, in other words, reflected the contemporary reality, not a backward one, for 'subaltern histories do not refer to a resistance prior and exterior to capital'.[11] This is also why the essays, as pointed out earlier, do not go to a time earlier than the 18th century.

By positing the peasant as part of modernity, subaltern studies challenged notions of the elite leadership 'taking' India to freedom and modernity. Colonialism itself created the structures of modernity, and there were multiple reactions to it. It was obviously difficult to find sources for such history writing. To find these sources, the subaltern group began to try and use different methods of reading the available documents, i.e. to read them 'against their grain'. For this purpose, they found the postmodern and postcolonial methodology useful. Subaltern studies brought in intensive study of archival material from a new perspective, while also exploring other sources, such as oral traditions, in order to try to uncover the aspect of memory mentioned above. They also began to use the methods of critical theory to try and deconstruct texts. They agreed that while peasants are not normally known for leaving behind their own sources, it was not necessary to give up archival sources in favour of methodologies of other disciplines, such as anthropology, sociology or demography. Instead, what was required was 'reading between the lines' of the existing archival material, and using other methodologies whenever necessary – for example, to try and understand the word 'riot' as used in the archival sources, one would have to go into literary theory. It was argued that it was possible to understand the nature of peasant consciousness through such intensive reading.

Ranajit Guha retired from the editorial team of Subaltern Studies in 1988. As mentioned earlier, shortly after he retired, an anthology entitled *Selected Subaltern Studies*, edited jointly by Guha and Gayatri Spivak, was published. It was perhaps from this time that the Subaltern Studies Project could be said to have attracted attention from academics all over the world, as can be seen from the foreword to the volume written by Edward Said.[12]

Criticism of the project had begun to appear a few years earlier. In 1984, the journal, *Social Scientist*, brought out a special issue devoted to subaltern studies. Among the charges levelled then were those of positivism and of not using the Marxist methodology 'properly'. It was elsewhere argued that though the subaltern scholars talked of the problem of sources, they were finally using the same sources in the same archives, and so, their approach was as subjective as those whom they challenged. They started with the idea that subalterns were autonomous in the Indian nationalist movement and actively participated in negotiating their situation. However, it was pointed out that in the process of finding these subaltern voices, they started examining instead the process of production of colonial knowledge, which then led them into directions far removed from their original ideas. These directions included examining the ideas of 'difference', and so, to 'provincialise Europe'[13] and then deconstruct history. However, the subalterns tended to lump together all those whom they defined as 'subaltern' as one oppressed mass of people so that it was difficult to see how the idea of difference could be constructed. It was pointed out by Rosalind O'Hanlon in 1988[14] that issues of gender were totally missing. Both O'Hanlon and Spivak also argued that the theoretical orientation of the project was limited for it was predicated, not on the idea of giving voice to the subaltern, but on 'letting the subaltern speak'.[15]

Some of these issues were addressed by the subaltern group, in particular by Dipesh Chakrabarty, in an article in *Subaltern Studies IV*, but on the whole, the approach at that time did not attract much attention, especially outside India.

Criticism of the project increased in the 1990s. Sumit Sarkar, earlier part of the project, was at the forefront of this criticism. He argued, among other things, that the project had given up the Marxist critique, which formed the basis of the earlier volumes, in favour of a "rejection of Enlightenment rationalism".[16] This, he felt, was particularly dangerous, for implied in the subaltern volumes was "the assumption that all really dangerous or meaningful forms of power [were] located uniquely in the modern state, whereas power within communities matter[ed] much less".[17] This is only part of the criticism, for the Subaltern Studies Project has now become part of the ongoing debate between Marxists and postmodernists. Early subaltern historiography argued against the idea of leadership, but talked of peasant movements. One criticism levelled against them is that a 'movement' by definition involves an ideology, and leadership, and mobilization around these two. When ideology is unclear (other than the general one of being against oppression), then mobilization has to be around a leader. Critics of the subaltern school argued that on the one hand, they talked of 'spontaneous' movements, and on the other, focussed on leaders of peasant (or any other) resistance, like Birsa Munda or Jitu Santhal. Even more important, it is pointed out that it is difficult to talk of peasant consciousness as being specifically anti-colonial. The subaltern scholars have themselves identified peasant resistance under the Mughals, the Marathas, and the British. Is this a clear 'peasant consciousness', or a more general consciousness of domination, and thus a reaction to authority itself? Further, it is argued that, as subaltern history is by definition 'fragmented' and 'episodic', academic studies that focus on the fragmentary would tend to deny the basic unity of all the oppressed. Oppression exists, and needs to be tackled on a number of levels. Theories which separate the different segments that constitute the oppressed would, in the long run, help only the forces of domination, for the dominant would be helped in their project of the subordinated by the fact of disunity among the oppressed. Sumit Sarkar pointed out that the subaltern approach could then be subsumed within Hindu fundamentalism.

In defence of the position of the subaltern studies group, it has been pointed out that the unity that the Marxists are trying to create is artificial. Fragmentation is everywhere in the world, now a part of the political reality, and the attempts of the Marxists to reduce all forms of oppression to gender, class, and ethnicity (or any or all of these), is finally defeating the cause of the oppressed. Subaltern histories, on the contrary, tried to "engage philosophically with questions of difference which are elided in the dominant traditions of Marxism".[18] Far from helping the cause of extremism, and thus rejecting democracy and social justice, the academics of the Subaltern Studies Project argue that the process of theorization of the fragments help to understand the nature of the groups involved and, therefore, in the long run, would help to achieve a more equitable social world. Only by 'taking history to its limits' would the 'unworking' be made 'visible'.[19] The subaltern approach studies, first of all, the nature of the subaltern's relation to the world, then the responses to it, and so studies the ways in which the relationship is sought to be improved. In other words, by studying the responses of the subalterns to the various aspects of their reality, one is better able to understand what it is that they are struggling for. It is only when this is understood that a genuine attempt can be made to improve the position of the subaltern.

Notes

1. A. Gramsci, *Selections from the Prison Notebooks*, (ed. and tr.) Quintin Hoare and Geoffrey Newell Smith, Orient Longman, 1996, pp. 54-55.
2. D. Chakrabarty, 'Invitation to a Dialogue', in R. Guha (ed.), *Subaltern Studies IV: Writings on South Asian History and Society*, Oxford India Paperbacks (henceforth OIP), Delhi, 1994, p. 373.
3. R. Guha, 'The Small Voice of History', in Shahid Amin and Dipesh Chakrabarty (eds.), *Subaltern Studies IX: Writings on South Asian History and Society*, OIP, Delhi, 1997, p. 1.
4. R. Guha, 'On Some Aspects of the Historiography of Colonial India', in R. Guha (ed.), *Subaltern Studies I: Writings on South Asian History and Society*, Oxford University Press (henceforth OUP), Delhi, 1982, p. 1.
5. Ibid., pp. 2-3.
6. Ibid., p. 3. Emphasis in the original.
7. R. Guha (ed.), *Subaltern Studies III: Writings on South Asian History and Society*, OUP, Delhi, 1984, Preface, p. vii.
8. For a more detailed exposition of the question of myth and memory, see Ajay Skaria, 'Some Aporias of History - Time, Truth and Play in Dangs, Gujarat', in *Economic and Political Weekly* (henceforth *EPW*), April 10, 1999, pp. 897-904.
9. Dipesh Chakrabarty, 'Marx after Marxism: A Subaltern Historian's Perspective', in *EPW*, May 20, 1993, p. 1096.
10. Gayatri Chakravorty Spivak, 'Subaltern Studies: Deconstructing Historiography', in R. Guha (ed.) *Subaltern Studies IV: Writings on South Asian History and Society*, p. 243.
11. Dipesh Chakrabarty, 'Marx after Marxism', op. cit.
12. R. Guha and Gayatri Chakravorty Spivak (eds.), *Selected Subaltern Studies*, OUP, 1988. Edward Said termed the project 'intellectually insurrectionary' – ibid., foreword, p. v.
13. This phrase is part of the title of a recently published book in 'Provincialising Europe'.
14. Rosalind O'Hanlon, 'Recovering the Subject: Subaltern Studies and Histories of Resistance in Colonial South Asia', in *Modern Asian Studies*, 22, No. 1, 1988, pp. 189-224.
15. Gayatri Chakravorty Spivak, 'Can the Subaltern Speak?', in P. Williams and L. Christian (eds.), *Colonial Discourse and Postcolonial Theory: A Reader*, Columbia University Press, 1994, pp. 66-111, cited

in Dipesh Chakrabarty, *Habitations of Modernity: Essays in the Wake of Subaltern Studies*, Permanent Black, Delhi, 2002, p. 17.

16. Sumit Sarkar, 'The Fascism of the Sangh Parivar', *EPW*, 20 January 1993, p. 167.
17. Sumit Sarkar, *Writing Social History*, OUP, Delhi, 1997, p. 10.
18. Dipesh Chakrabarty, 'Marx after Marxism', op. cit., p. 1096.
19. Ibid.

9

Postmodernism and History

C.R. Das

The world today is often described in academic circles as the postmodern world or the world of postmodernism. To begin with, postmodernism may be viewed as mostly an intellectual phenomenon and is an extremely complex phenomenon to be characterized as such. By implication, it refers to a specific temporality in the Western world simultaneous with post-industrial. It is not possible to specify where 'modern' ends and 'postmodern' begins or whether postmodern is a continuation of modernity and, therefore, in a sense, an internal critique of the culture of modernity. In any case, it may be safe to propose postmodernism here as a certain critique of the culture of modernity. It interrogates modernity in all its manifestations. That is where the strength of its existence really lies. Although it has not yet produced any alternative system or apparatus by way of methodology or model, which can be considered a viable alternative to the modernist model, it continues to occupy centrestage in current academic thinking, for it has raised questions that hit at the core of modernist thinking.

The modern (Western) civilization has produced and sustained itself through a variety of activities, which include inter alia, philosophical systems, specific ideological thrusts, institutional arrangements, and academic systems. Academic systems that modernity has produced and has been able to sustain over a period of three centuries or so have to be seen in the forms of academic philosophy, institutional arrangements, the state-academic alliance, and the culture begotten of it. The disciplinary focus of the modernist academic project, with clearly demarcated boundaries of the academic disciplines into self-contained disciplines with resources such as theory, methodology, and conceptual grid, has carried forward with its thrust on academic production through specific approaches of each discipline, bound however by common commitment to science or the 'scientific'. Scientific approach, disciplinary norms, professionalization of disciplines, and state funding have constituted the various sides of the academic approach and practices from the 19th century onwards.

Origin

Perry Anderson traces the lengthy provenance of postmodernism in cosmopolitanism, a multimedia affair that began in the field of architecture and carried into the fields of arts and humanities. The idea of postmodernism surfaced in the Hispanic inter-world of the 1930s. Federico de Onis used the term 'postmodernismo' for the first time. It was in 1950s that the term emerged in the anglophone world as an epochal, rather than aesthetic, category. Arnold Toynbee in his *Study of History* (1934) had argued the rise of deep hostility to nationalism, suspicion of industrialism and decolonization, and it was in his eighth volume, published in 1954, that he dubbed the epoch that had opened with the Franco-Prussian War as the 'postmodern age'. While it is not possible to pinpoint the origins of any movement exactly in time, in the case of postmodernism, it can be said that it began with the blowing up of a building, designed in the Le Corbusierian School, St. Louis, Missouri, at 3:32 PM on July 15, 1972. It announced the end of rationalist utopia, a dream of a planned and 'rectangular' world, which could replace the turmoil and economic depression of the 1930s. The marginality of the modernist artist, which was connected with elitism, is now incorporated into the daily existence of a capitalist society in which Fordism is out and small-scale production is the order of the day. We are in the age of Derrida in a new phase of multicultural capitalism with its ceaseless circulation of information, codes, and signs. It is the age of the 'signifier in isolation', a reality that it built on a collective make-believe world where fiction and reality merge together, producing a collage city with its populist and decentred architecture, where you cannot find your way out, a contrast to the monastic austerity of modernism, which based itself on the user-friendly notion of all creation. The city cannot be totalized now.

What is Postmodernism/Postmodernity

Postmodernism may be summarized as a series of reactions to the culture of the modern West within the larger context of late capitalism, consumerism, politics of identity, paradigm shift in scientific epistemology (from Newtonian atomistic mathematical certainty to Einstenian relativism and uncertain science), postcolonial and diasporic consciousness and multiculturalism and discovery of indigeneity. The terms 'modern' and 'postmodern' refer to broad social and cultural patterns or sensibilities that can be analytically distinguished for the purpose of highlighting social trends. In art and architecture, we can point to the surfacing of the postmodern in styles and the collapse of hierarchical distinction between high art and popular art. Signs of postmodernity are visible in processes of 'de-differentiation' (the breakdown between social institutions and cultural spheres) and the 'de-territorialization' of national economies and cultures.

The centrality of constructions of the world, self, and society in the modernist paradigm have come under critical scrutiny. The Enlightenment, which is at the heart of Western modernity, is facing a deep-rooted challenge to its epistemic authority. Assumptions regarding the unity of humanity, the individual as the creative force of society and history, the superiority of the West, the idea of science as Truth, and the belief in social progress so fundamental to Western modernity have been put under critical scrutiny.

For some Marxist interpreters, postmodernism is the arrival of the end of capitalism. For apologists of capitalism, postmodernity is the permanent arrival of capitalism and has a basis in the geopolitical world order, a result predictable from the premises of market capitalism. Taken together, both are seamlessly predictable and mutually contradictory. What does seem widely agreeable is that postmodernism is a historical term, and that it indicates whatever comes after modernity. The burden of definition then shifts to where it belongs, to the question: What is 'modern'? Some conflate 'modern' with 'postmodern' and thus limit attention to a fairly local event around the turn of the 20th century. Others use 'modern' to indicate post-Enlightenment, the era since the late 18th century. Still others, especially historians, use 'modern' to indicate 'post-mediaeval', or the culture distinct from and subsequent to that of the Middle Ages. For these writers, 'modernity' as a culture of humanist rationality was constructed and disseminated in Renaissance Europe. Postmodernity is whatever succeeds that modernity.

Postmodernity has also been seen as a challenge to modernity and its philosophical and epistemological premises. Challenges to assumptions underlying modernity began well before the 20th century. Non-Euclidean geometry appeared before the middle of the 19th century, as did the science leading to Maxwell's equations; in fact, Andre Breton congratulated the entire 19th century for denouncing the ridiculous illusion of happiness and understanding that accompanied the Enlightenment Smile of Reason. In 1905, Einstein's special theory of relativity constituted a determining step away from the settled empiricist assumptions in science; in 1907, Picasso's 'Demoiselles d'Avignon' marked developments away from the representational agendas that were producing a turning point in the history of art; and in the same decade (1906-1911), Ferdinand de Saussure was giving lectures at Geneva that inspired a revolutionary shift away from related agendas in the theory of knowledge. In subsequent decades, the failure of representational politics produced and reproduced world wars. Since the turn of the 20th century, these and other changes in knowledge and other expectations have worked together to unsettle the assumption basic to what is called the 'culture of representation', including especially its development in Europe of democratic institutions and their 'individual' agents.

The assumptions in question have to do with the definition and stability of individual identity and (this is essential) the correlative objectivity of the world. The 'individual' agent of modernity exists for and makes possible the 'objectivity' that we have learned to take for granted, thanks to our familiarity with representational conventions first in art, then in science, and then in political systems. During the 20th century, substantial changes to that culture have been sufficient to produce a massive self-examination across cultural systems, from science to politics, from art to economics.

Postmodern themes seem especially visible in the realm of knowledge. For example, disciplinary boundaries are blurring and new interdisciplinary, hybrid knowledges such as feminism, lesbianism and gay studies, ethnic studies, urban studies, and cultural studies are moving to the centre of human studies. The lines between science, literature, and ideology, between literature and literary criticism, between philosophy and cultural criticism, between high cultural criticism and popular criticism, have blurred considerably, much to the dismay of the defenders of the Enlightenment culture. As disciplinary boundaries and the line between science and non-science blur, as claims to universal knowledge lack credibility, as knowledges are viewed as interlaced with rhetoric and power, the very meaning of knowledge is changing.

The 'postmodern turn' refers to challenges to the Enlightenment paradigm of social knowledge. Its purpose is to survey proposals to rethink human studies. This postmodern knowledge contests disciplinary boundaries, the separation of science, literature, and ideology, and the division between knowledge and power.

Zygmunt Bauman sketches a shift from modernity to postmodernity. The former, according to Bauman, is characterized by the dominance of a culture of control seen in the form of imposing order through categorizing, classifying, and regulating nature and humanity. This is an era organized around the search for general principles, laws of mind, society, and history, and the quest for certainty and foundations. Postmodernity features a process of de-differentiation or the collapse of boundaries and loss of an epistemic and social centre. The social world is fragmented into a multitude of communities, cultural traditions, and knowledges. The languages of detached observers, objectivity, universality, and truth passes into a culture organized around the irreducible plurality of knowledges and standpoints and the intermingling of knowledge, rhetoric, and politics.

History as a Discipline

The discipline of history emerged in the modern Western cultural ambience. The discipline of history is modern not only because it originated in the present form in the 18th century, but because it has been looked upon as part of the modernist project implicated in the politics of modernity also. The emergence and growth of history as a discipline has much to do with the entire epistemology that the Enlightenment modernity produced with its thrust on the notion of 'scientific' as incorporated in the philosophy and methodology of empiricist, rationalist, and positivist scientific epistemology and enquiry. The 'empiricist, positivist (social) science puts its methodological premium on 'objectivity', 'universality', 'verifiability', and 'testability', which of necessity conformed to the notions of 'progress' and 'teleology'. The role of agency in explaining social phenomena assumed great significance in the light of a scientific explanatory thrust. Political history with its emphasis on the role of state, political institutions, and big personalities attempted to narrate historical phenomena in a evolutionary, historical, and diachronic manner. It catered to or served the requirements of the emergent nation-state. The entire historical narrative was based on authenticated historical documents, which comprised, as Ranke emphasized, state papers, diplomatic correspondence, biography, and autobiography of prominent personalities, etc. 'No document, no history' characterized the spirit of historical research as stressed by Charles Seignobos. In a nutshell, the idea was that explaining political agency, its role, and the consequences of actions performed by 'rational agency' was tantamount to the entire historical explanation of a particular period of history (the periodization of which was done accordingly). The objectives of history (political history) got entangled with the objectives of the nation-state. In a way, it was the nation-state that provided the framework for writing the history of states and nations. In brief, traditional history, especially 'classical political history', was based on the concept of 'subject': The subjectivity of historical agents was rational and autonomous; the subject was a preconstituted centre and, therefore, actions were caused and fully explained by the intentions that motivated them.

Social history, on the contrary, was based on the concept of society. For social historians, subjectivity and culture are not rational creations, but representations or expressions of the social context in which the causes of actions were to be found. However, since the social historians had to face the explanatory anomalies of this schemata, they were compelled to make more flexible the causal link between social structure and conscious actions, to attribute to agents an active role in the production of meanings and to grant a relative autonomy to the cultural sphere. Social historians tended to explain cultural meanings and social practice only in economic and social terms. In this explanatory schema, culture was treated as a simple function of the social. Social historians maintain(ed) that any action is undoubtedly a response to the pressure and requirements of the social context. In brief, for social history, since the agents' conscious actions are no more than expressions of their social context, the aim of historical enquiry is to reconstruct that context.

The project of history based on the modernist epistemological assumptions was primarily located in rationalism, empiricism, and positivism. It accepted the 'correspondence theory' of truth. Language was viewed as only a medium of representation. It claimed to be scientific because of its adherence to the rigour of objectivity, rational explanatory schema, mathematization and context and value-free engagement and canonization. The philosophical developments in the West (Europe) in the 18th and 19th centuries, designated as 'Enlightenment' and also 'post-Enlightenment', provided the basic scheme for its explanatory framework in the form of the linear conception of time, the paradigm of 'continuity and change', 'progress', 'rise and fall (decline)', 'end of history', etc. Historical science in this framework became a continuous search for universal patterns. 'Local' got connected with the universal. The search and discovery of the universal in the particular and 'unique particular' in the universal came to characterize the spirit of historical research till the Annales School came into being. Grand narratives of nation states became mainstream history. Epistemologically, methodologically, conceptually, heuristically and thematically, the disciplinary practice of history was a product and handiwork of the Western 'modernity'.

Keeping in view the above brief presentation of modernity, it would be worthwhile to look at some of the interesting issues raised by postmodernity with particular reference to the discipline of history. Postmodernism raises several issues about the disciplinary practices of history.

History as a discipline is viewed by postmodernism as a project of modernity. As such, it caters to the requirements of modernity. Postmodernism is understood here as a continuous interrogation of modernity that challenges its very epistemological foundations. Behind the entire modus of modernity as the most celebrated system, postmodernism sees a power structure. Therefore, modernity is viewed as the Western 'myth' that continues to sustain the power structure and perpetuates modernity. A brief review of some of these issues as raised by Foucault, Derrida, Lyotard, and Barthes would suffice here.

1. For Foucault, there is no unmediated access for the human mind to a genuinely knowable original and truthful reality. Our only door to experience (past, present, and future) is through the primary medium of language as a signifying process normally constituted within a framework for the exercise of power, legitimacy, and illegitimacy. Derived from Nietzsche, this is a fundamental shift from empiricism, because it entertains the impossibility of knowing anything objectively, given that objectivity itself is a historical and cultural construct. The postmodernist idea of mediation, has been of great significance. This is with direct reference to the empiricist and positivist notion of language which views language as merely a carrier and as playing no other role. Language in the new theoretical proposition, not only reflects, but refracts also, depending on the density of the medium. The 'performatory' role of language has come to replace its earlier roles. According to this, there is no direct one-to-one correspondence between the word and the world. Language mediates and generates meaning. The relation between the word and the world is not direct, but mediated. Given the new role of language, the concept of discourse has come to play a significant role in the making of the meaning of a text. A text of history, in this sense, loses its earlier scientific moorings and becomes a text

open to various interpretations. What has been of great significance within the Foucauldian intervention is the idea of discursive mediation. Foucault shifts the entire focus of understanding from a pure positivistic scientific insistence to operation of discourse and discursive mediation. There is an emerging trend in social science researches today, particularly in history, which focus on the discursive aspects of academic production.

2. Historical constructions have clearly been guided by the ideas of progress and teleology. The concept of progress has been derived from the evolutionary sciences of the 19th century and, as used in historical narratives, has always created a narrative of progress from the lower order to the higher order, from an imperfect condition towards a perfect condition, through a process of higher attainments (more distinct in liberal historiography). It postulates an idea of the future, a state of imagined (ideologically) perfect condition and, above all, a 'continuity' and 'transition'. In Marxist historiography, such a linear course of historical progress is guided by its own inherent logic.

   Like Vico, White and Foucault both accept the creative power of language. The complex manner in which we use language and language uses us to mediate past reality suggests that no amount of sophistication in a social science can avoid the interactive relationship between the historian, the word, and the world. A narrative is not simply the representation of past reality, but a reproduction of the relation subsisting between them. Language is primarily a creative medium that has the power to invent and create our knowledge of the past.

3. Foucault's intention of undermining logocentrism was eventually exemplified in his model of the rhetorically and socially constructed episteme. It was his aim to locate the means by which knowledge is produced linguistically within society. In doing this, unlike most historians who

view change over time as the discovery of the linear or diachronic unfolding of coherent narrative or interconnected process, Foucault views it as a network or synchronic structure of power relationship, the aim of which is to create knowledge, and in so doing, particular historical knowledge. As he insists, history is not about factual discovery, but about the literary and textual creation of knowledge for the purpose of the exercise of power, or to counter such exercise as a form of literary dissent.

4. Foucault is highly critical of the historians' search for origin. Instead, he suggests that they must now try to understand, explain, and interpret the operation and existence of power structures that were behind all historical models or epistemologies. His 'genealogical' and 'archaeological' methods have charted new history. In his early works, Foucault makes metaphoric use of 'archaeology'. The metaphor of archaeology suggests that Foucault was attempting an excavation of knowledge, a search for its underlying conditions and determinants. Archaeology follows structuralism in the search for underlying rules of human thought and knowledge. Another of Foucault's important methods is called 'genealogy'. He characterizes his 'genealogy' as a new mode of historical writing, calling genealogists as 'the new historians'. Both archaeology and genealogy attempt to reexamine the social field from a micrological standpoint that enables one to identify discursive discontinuity and dispersion, instead of continuity and identity, and to grasp 'events' in their real complexity.
5. The first challenge to the way narrative and the rhetoric of history were conceived of in the modernist schema, came from Roland Barthes between 1966 and 1968. Barthes posed a fundamental question: Does history differ in some identifiable and important way from fictional narrative? Barthes made a formal analysis of historical writing and rejected root and branch historical realism.

6. Narrative is history's primary cognitive device working in the mind of the historians – she imagines, shapes, and represents the past. The 'emplotment' (Hayden White) of history as a story, with its supporting arguments and ethical strategies of explanation of historical change, is not history as it actually happened. How the past is configured hangs on the historian's capacity to match a type of emplotment with the historical events that she wishes to furnish with a meaning of a particular kind. Hayden White talked of tropes such as 'metaphor', 'metonymy', 'synecdoche', and 'irony', and four modes of emplotment such as the 'romantic', 'tragic', 'comic', and 'satiric'. White viewed that the four kinds of trope, which act as the foundation for all historical interpretation, are four kinds of explanation in three tiers, namely, four emplotments associated with four types of arguments such as 'formist' 'mechanistic', 'organicist', and 'contextualist', and four idealogical positions such as 'anarchism', radicalism', 'conservatism', and 'liberalism'. White's formalist theory of historical narrative offers a morphology for a study of the past. Historical understanding, according to White, is derived from evidence that lies not at the level of individual referential statement, but its emplotted arrangement. Narrative explanation is more than recording a flow of events in their order of occurrence. The historian's function, noted by Gallie as the essence of historical understanding, is to offer a story that is followable. Such followability emerges when the stories that the historians tell are coherent and appear plausible in the light of the available evidence. The reality of the past does not already exist in the unhewn marble, requiring only the historian's skill to chip away to reveal the object existing within. White argues that history is a tropically prefigured literary artefact, a story as much invented as found.

7. Foucault and White offer the figurative process as a model through which historical change is lived and can be explained. 'Naïve realism' does not take sufficient notice of the great power of 'language not only to describe but also to invent'. Empiricism necessarily sells history short. As White says, language used to describe a field of historical occurences in effect constitutes the field itself and, therefore, limits the kind of methods that can be used to 'analyse the events occurring within the field'. This great power of language resides in its metaphoric and figurative (tropological) structure. The historical narrative 'does not image the thing it indicates; it calls to mind images of things it indicates'. In other words, the metaphor cannot constitute a genuine image of the object it aspires to describe, and offers instead a cognitive map for the reader to find the appropriate (and explanatory) associative images.
8. The postmodern critique does not accept the idea of linear and progressive historical rhythm tagged to teleology. In the place of progressive historical narrative, it introduces the idea of discontinuity, disjuncture, interruption, etc. (Foucault). Derrida's anti-foundationalism strongly opposes the Enlightenment Reason, which is at the heart of such epistemologies.
9. Serious critiques of history derive from Lyotard's distinction between a pre-modern fluid, free, popular universe of narrativizatiom in the form of story-telling, and the abstract world of modern professionalized, 'scientific' discourses (including history) that perpetually seek legitimisation through argument and debate. This has raised a distinction between history and myth, and has foregrounded the idea of authenticity and true history.
10. For Lyotard, modern and scientific discourses are objectionable and inevitably power ridden primarily because they are 'foundational', grounded in grand and meta-narratives. The projected alternative is local knowledge, a valorisation of fragments.

11. Postmodernism is critical of the explanatory historical schema in terms of causes and effects, called 'effective' history. 'Effective' history is based upon the principles of 'necessity' and 'sufficiency'. Sufficient number of causes fulfilling the minimum causal explanatory requirements satisfy a historical explanatory schema. An attempt at accounting for a historical 'event' does little for the 'surplus'.
12. Recent years have witnessed a somewhat ambiguous coming together of philosophy and history, as the truth claims of both have come under trenchant scrutiny through a linguistic-cum-literary turn, which has tried to invert the traditional primacy of logic over rhetoric. Emanating from new forms of literary theory, this critique seeks to blur genre distinctions between literature, philosophy, and indeed all disciplines, and grants to literary criticism, in Habermas' words, 'an almost world historical mission' to seek out and destroy the metaphysics of presence everywhere. Herein lies one major constituent of what, conveniently, if vaguely, have come to be called postmodernist moods.

Postmodernism has challenged the very knowledge foundations and basic premises of modernity. The scientific claims of modernity and its entire productive mechanism in the forms of disciplinary practices have been seriously questioned. History has been viewed as an instrument of ideological control (by a class). The scientific status of history has been seriously challenged and history has been viewed as a discourse and instrument of hegemony. The discipline has been a part of the same modernist representational politics and the entire modernist cognitive resources have occluded the marginalized from history. Such challenges are seen at the level of methodological practices, forms of presentation, and scientific pretences. The historical methodologies, including its insistence only on written sources and representational and explanatory techniques, have led to elitism within history. The 'postmodernist turn', therefore, tries to critically locate such history, including its crafts, in a structure of power relations. Its insistence on understanding the underlying power structure and going beyond written sources and elite historiography has led to a great deal of theoretical modification, ethno-historical engagement, multidisciplinary research, conceptual rigour, and local history epistemological exercises by blurring genres and, above all, cognitive restoration. The most important effect of the postmodernist interrogation of history has been in the form of the emergence of 'the new cultural history' with new theorization of 'identity', 'experience', and 'interest' and the emergence of a new social theory. The subaltern turn in historiography may have to be placed in this direction.

Further Readings

Ankersmith, F.R., *History and Tropology: The Rise and Fall of Metaphor*, University of California Press, Berkeley, 1994.

Barthes, Roland, *Mythologies*, Jonathan Cape, London, 1972.

—, *The Semiotic Challenge*, Basil Blackwell, UK, 1988.

Burke, Peter (ed.), *New Perspectives on Historical Writing*, Cambridge University Press, Cambridge, 1991.

de Saussure, Ferdinand, *Course da Linguistic Generale* (1916), (tr.) Wade Baskin, Fontana, London, 1959.

Derrida, Jacques, *Of Gramattology*, (tr.) G.C. Spivak, Johns Hopkins University Press, Baltimore, 1976.

Elton, G.R., *The Practice of History*, Crowell, 1967.

Foucault, Michel, *The Archaeology of Knowledge*, Harper and Row, New York, 1972.

—, *The Order of Things: An Archaeology of Human Sciences*, Random House, New York, 1973.

Gallie, W.B., *Philosophy and The Historical Understanding*, Schocken Books, New York, 1968.

Habermass, Jurgen, *Philosophical Discourses of Modernity*, Cambridge, 1997.

Iggers, Georg, *New Directions in European Historiography* (revised edition), Methuen and Co., London, 1985.

Joseph, Sarah, *Interrogating Culture: Critical Perspectives on Contemporary Social Theory*, Sage, 1998.

Kuhn, T.S., *The Structure of Scientific Revolutions*, University of Chicago Press, Chicago, 1961.

Ludden, David (ed.), *Reading Subaltern Studies: Critical History, Contested Meaning, and the Globalization of South Asia*, Permanent Black, New Delhi, 2001.

Marwick, Arthur, *The Nature of History*, Macmillan, London, 1989.

Munslow, Alun, *Deconstructing History*, Routledge, New York, 1997.

Norris, Christopher, *Deconstruction: Theory and Practice*, Methuen, London, 1982.

Popper, Karl , *The Logic Of Scientific Discovery*, Hutchinson, London, 1959.

Recoeur, Paul, *History and Truth*, 4th edition, (edited and translated with Introduction by Charles A. Kelbley), North Western University Press, 1992.

Seidman, Steven (ed.), *The Postmodern Turn: New Perspectives on Social Theory*, Cambridge, 1994.

White, Hayden, *Metahistory: Historical Imagination in the Nineteenth Century*, Johns Hopkins University Press, Baltimore, 1973.

Journals/Periodicals

'Agency after Postmodernism' *History and Theory: Studies in the Philosophy of History*, in Theme Issue 40, (Number 4, December 2001), Wesleyan University, USA.

History of the Human Sciences, Vol. 15, No. 1, February 2002, Sage London, Thousand Oaks, and New Delhi.

Walia, Shelly, 'Antinomies of Postmodernity', *Biblio*, May-June 1999, pp. 19-20.

10

The Regional Conception of History

An Introductory Essay

Umesh A. Kadam

Historians are rarely conscious that in their primary function of collecting and interpreting facts contained in records from the past, they use concepts and categories that need definition and clarification for correct and complete comprehension of the scenario they describe. Even standard works on history of any period or people take for granted that the reader is well familiar with the full meaning of the various concepts and processes used in constructing the past of the period or the people concerned. This problem is further compounded when a single term used in historical sources of different periods and localities has different meanings or varying shades thereof with practically no resemblance to the meaning we attribute in our own time. However, our concern here is not with technical terms in historical sources, but with types in historiography. In a country of subcontinental size like India, focus on distinctive features of its various parts is as much significant as viewing the country as a whole. Thus, identifying their various parts in terms of region as a unit of historical research is not as easy as it might seem. Before undertaking research in the history of an area taken to be a distinct region, it is essential to satisfy oneself whether it contains all or most of the elements that go into the making of a region.

Though as a concept, region is common to all social sciences, it is often overlooked that contributions to building theory and methodology in the field have come as much from physical sciences as from social ones. A section of biologists, for example, differs from physiologists on the subject of man-land relationship. If a human being is taken to be a political animal in agreement with Aristotle, adding the corollary that a sense of belonging to a piece of territory renders her also a territorial animal, then the roots of regionalism could be located in human nature itself. The biological basis could also be pointed out citing the cases of insects, rodents, birds, and even mammals (higher apes), which run into rage, offering bitter resistance against their own species in the course of defending the territory they inhabit. Traversing from biology to sociology, one could say that the defining features of a region are as much god-made as human-made. It is a human being who moulds the land to her own purposes and brings out, in the process, its distinct individuality. Its multiple separate features get integrated in the course of human activities that "substitute for the incoherent effect of local circumstances a systematic concourse of forces. It is thus that a region defines and differentiates itself and becomes as it were a medal struck off in the effigy of a people".

This distinct individuality, demarcating a region from its neighbouring ones, consists of the cultural forms and social systems handed down from its hoary past. Any study in the field, therefore, must trace the roots of regional identity to its articulation in modern times. In the Indian situation, the transition from a tribal system of social organization to the peasantization of the population under evolving state systems of impersonal control did not occur in all parts of the country simultaneously. This law of uneven development is well reflected in the continuously changing configuration of core areas under direct state control and peripheral areas experiencing indirect political hegemony, and this interplay between the two found its clear manifestation on the cultural plane. The history of Indian temple architecture documenting the development of various regional styles is a case in point. On the religious plane, the notion of bhakti, pleading for worship of an individualized deity, and the avatar theory resulted in a sort of cultural osmosis. In the sociopolitical context, the invention of mythologies and fabrication of genealogies contributed to the flourishing of countless little traditions under the umbrella of a great tradition. It is evident, therefore, in the Indian context that regional histories have singular importance and serve as a corrective in respect of the generalization given to us in colonial as well as postcolonial times.

Regional historiography in India has been motivated by the nationalist school and its writings. In many parts of India, regional history is being taught as an important segment of the history syllabus. History as a subject cannot be isolated from other disciplines. History nowadays is becoming more of an interdisciplinary subject. Moreover, history has to be studied and well researched in the time and space context. Chronology and geography are considered to be the two eyes of history. While performing preliminary operations on a particular topic, the historian has to take into account the geographical setting of the region.

A lot of groundwork towards the development of regional history has been done by the Annales School. This school first made its appearance in 1929. Annalism has since played a decisive role in dictating the agenda of 20th century history writing. Neopositivists like Lucien Febvre and Marc Bloch are known to be the founders of this school. Febvre, Bloch and Fernand Braudel have contributed a lot towards the development of this school. Inspired by their model, other leading historians like Francois Furet, Emmaneul Le Roy-Ladurie and Jacques Rene also adopted the multidisciplinary approach. They have constructed history mainly upon the four main pillars of geography, demography, sociology, and economics. Febvre and Bloch drew primarily upon sociology, economic history, literature, and psychology, but Braudel tapped into another rich French historical tradition, geography. Braudel says, "Mountains, as much as money, make the Man."

The Oxford Dictionary defines region as a continuous part of a surface, space, or body; an administrative division of a country. 'History' means investigation. If we combine these two words to understand as one 'concept', then the meaning changes altogether. Regional history can mean investigation of a region or investigation of the administrative division of a country. If such a meaning of regional history is formulated, then it will limit the scope of research. Both history as well as region does constitute many factors to form their own identity. This means region constitutes not only the geography, natural elements, and the demography, but also the society and its relation with the environment. The interaction thus forms socioeconomic and political identities. These identities are broadly called 'cultural units'.

Culture is a very ambiguous concept. Some anthropologists consider culture to be social behaviour. For others, it is not behaviour at all, but an abstraction from behaviour. To some, stone axes and pottery, dance and music, fashion and style constitute culture, while no material object can be culture to others; for some, culture exists only in the mind. One of the oldest definitions of culture was given by the British anthropologist, Sir E.B. Taylor (1832-1917) in the opening lines of his book, *Primitive Cultures* (1871). He says, "Culture is that complex whole which includes knowledge, belief, art, morals, law, customs, and other capabilities and habits acquired by man as a member of society." Margaret Mead (1901-1978) defines the concept thus: "Culture is the learned behaviour of a society or a sub-group." According to Raymond Williams (1921-1988), one of the founders of cultural studies, "Culture includes the organization of production, the structure of family, the structure of institutions which express or govern social relationships, the characteristic forms through which members of the society communicate." Clifford Geertz, Professor of Social Science at Princeton University says, "Culture is simply the ensemble of stories we tell ourselves about ourselves." On the basis of these definitions, culture seems to be (almost) everything and cultural studies the study of (almost) everything.

The world has witnessed, from times immemorial, the existence of such cultural units, their interaction with one another, and also the quest for keeping up their identities and offering required responses to all challenges. Regional history is thus an important instrument by which it will always be possible for us to measure the progress made by mankind. Regional history is becoming more and more popular, for it has the inherent potential of tapping a variety of sources for studying different aspects of history. Due to this, it merits the attention, not only of the specialists in the region, but also of historians working on other aspects of Indian history.

The scope of regional history is too vast; it cannot be studied in a summary manner. This paper limits itself towards understanding the development of regional history in India. When one works on the history of a region, the substance of problems she faces remains the same in most of the case studies, i.e. when a researcher is formulating the hypotheses. The hypotheses do help the scholar towards obtaining a clear understanding of the region and its history.

Indian history has been investigated by various schools, viz., imperialist, nationalist, Marxist, subaltern, and so on. These various schools of history have brought out different dimensions of understanding Indian history; moreover, their largest contribution is the mass of sources they have been able to tap. In their conventional form of presenting history, all these schools have brought out varied and very important information about the different regions in India. The painstaking efforts of these schools have produced political, economic, social, cultural and many other dimensions of the regional aspect. In other words, these schools have contributed indirectly to the development of regional histories and their importance in India. So, to have a proper understanding of the development of regional history, it must also be studied with reference to the various schools of history in India.

Early attempts at regional history were motivated primarily to locate new source material. This search has resulted in an abundance of sources, archaeological, epigraphical, historical literature, religious literature, archival records, and family papers, all of which have added to the body of information available on the history of many regions of the subcontinent. It is, however, at the interpretational level that the interest in regional history assumes greater historiographic potential, a potential with which we are perhaps as yet not altogether fully familiar.

The historical interest in regions such as South India, Bengal, and Maharashtra coincided with the new sources providing information, particularly on what came to be regarded as the inter-empire periods of Indian history or, alternatively, complementing the information available from the records outside the region. It began to be seen that the supposed Dark Ages stressed by the historiography of the 19th century were far from dark and that the lacunae could be eliminated by using local source material. It is in these inter-imperial periods that the nature of historical change at the regional level can be seen more clearly.

In the process, regional history becomes a corrective to the earlier tendency of generalizing about the subcontinent from the perspective of the Ganges Valley. Due to the spread of nationalism in the various states, there was increased interest in regional history. This interest brought its own perspective of the emergence of professional groups who participated in the national movement, and at the same time aspired to acquire an identity from the past. The tradition has continued into the post-independence period, as well. It can be argued that historical writing often takes the form of a desire to establish an identity on the part of the social group to which the historian belongs.

The histories related to the Maratha state in general and relating to the various elite factions of the Maratha state have projected the form of legitimization of the hegemonic status of the Chhatrapatis, Peshwas, and Karbharis and aristocrats such as the Shindes, Holkars, Gaikwads, Patwardhans, Nagpurkars, and Bhosales, etc. Groups in power, therefore, sometimes tend to see the history of the region or even of the nation as their own history, e.g., the histories of the Gaikwads of Gujarat, Shindes of Gwalior, Holkars of Indore, Peshwas of Pune and Bhosales of Nagpur are studied as regional histories at the micro level in particular in the sense of cultural units representing a certain peculiar culture of the region. On the other hand, all these histories are termed to be a single history of the Marathas in the context of the 'Maharashtra dharma', which represents the regional identity of all Marathi-speaking people, mostly having many common cultural customs practised all over Maharashtra.

To some scholars of Maratha history, the history of the Marathas is not restricted to the history of a certain cultural group or a certain linguistic group or a certain aristocratic group of the region. They also do not restrict it to the history of the Deccan; instead, they say that the 18th century history of India is mostly dominated by the Marathas. Hence, the 18th century history of India is nothing but the history of the Marathas. Thus, they attempt to project Maratha history to be a 'national history' at the macro level.

Groups in power, therefore, sometimes tend to see the history of their community as the history of the region or even of the nation. This is further emphasized in contemporary historical writing by the equating of the present-day state boundaries as the boundary of the region and this is held to be viable for all periods of history. A lot of attention has to be paid to the three trends cited by Romila Thapar in her address to the Punjab History Conference at Patiala in 1976. In her address on 'The Scope and Significance of Regional History', Thapar has used Punjab as a case study for understanding and constructing a regional history. She has drawn attention to three trends. Firstly, the acceptance of the conventional periodization of ancient, mediaeval, and modern.

Periodization does not merely imply time brackets; it also involves historical assumptions. The acceptance of this periodization imposes assumptions on the historical data from regional sources. Periodization must not be used as a convenience to suit the purpose, nor should it be allowed to become an intellectual truth. Secondly, the theories in vogue, believed to be almost axiomatic, must not be endorsed for understanding regional history. Thirdly, the inevitable search for a golden age traced by a dominant group, which is described in the glowing tints of cultural resurgence.

Regional history, if applied to Indian history, can play a catalytic role. It must not be subjected to the mere generalizations of Indian history. On the contrary, analysis of the historical patterns of the region must be studied. When a researcher begins with a region having a history, she tries to analyse the roots, i.e. administrative or political urges or a combination of many factors. For analysis, it is equally imperative to consider which preceded it and which came subsequently. The next important problem the researcher faces pertains to fixing the geographical boundaries of the region. This fixing of boundaries is a complex task in itself, for man-made boundaries change frequently and rapidly with political change. The only stable boundaries are geographical, and even these are liable to be substantially modified by ecological changes. The definition of a region requires the correlation of many facets in the study of historical evolution.

This can be demonstrated in the case of mediaeval Maratha country. Maratha country is broadly a part of the Deccan. Likewise, the demarcation of the region can be traced from the development of the 'Bhakti movement', from Dyaneshwar to Tukaram, on the basis of linguistic interaction and socioreligious and cultural patterns. It can also be defined as a geographical region, comprising three units, viz., 'Konkan' (seashore, ports, and their hinterlands), 'Ghat-matha' (mountain regions above sea level), and 'Desh' (plains). At the administrative level, the regional history can be divided into two units: Firstly, 'Swaraj', i.e. the Maratha country, and secondly, land (region) outside 'Swaraj'. The Marathas used to collect 'Sardeshmukhi' (one-tenth of land revenue) in the Swaraj, while Chauth (quarter of the total revenue) was collected from the adjoining the region or outside Swaraj.

Regional history has to be understood with a high level of objectivity. The element of subjectivity can reduce regional history into a hypocritical affair. Regional history must be researched in the proper context of the existing cultural patterns. Great care must be taken while comparing regions and formulating their analysis. Comparative studies would suggest the similarities within the two regions, thereby enabling a wider generalization. Dissimilarities would indicate the particular regional factors and would lead to a modification of the broader generalization.

Regional histories are histories of great and significant value. It is essentially due to them that new sources are added to the existing ones. Regional history sheds new light on the unknown sections of the society and their culture, thereby enriching our knowledge of the subaltern aspects of our societies. It strengthens the bonds between varied regions, by doing comparative and statistical analysis. Moreover, it also helps in understanding the modes of administration and urbanisation. Hence, the scope and significance of regional history is ever extending and broadening the horizons of historical knowledge.

Further Readings

Grewal, J.S., *Studies in Local and Regional History*, Guru Nanak Dev University, Amritsar, 1974.

Sills, David L. (ed.), *International Encyclopedia of Social Sciences*, Vol. 13, The Macmillan Co. and The Free Press, 1968.

Thapar, Romila, *Ancient Indian Social History: Some Interpretations*, Orient Longman, New Delhi, 1979.

Contributors

Kirit K. Shah, Professor and Head, University Department of History, S.N.D.T. Women's University, Mumbai.

Meherjyoti Sangle, Lecturer, University Department of History, S.N.D.T. Women's University, Mumbai.

Pushpa Bhave, Ex-Head, Department of Marathi, Ram Narayan Ruia College, Matunga, Mumbai.

Aniket Jaaware, Professor, Department of English, University of Pune, Pune.

Raja Dixit, Reader, Department of History, University of Pune, Pune.

Chhaya Goswami, Faculty Member, Department of History, Elphinstone College, Mumbai.

Aravind Ganachari, Reader, Department of History, University of Mumbai, Mumbai.

Jatin Wagle, Lecturer, Department of English, S.I.E.S. College of Arts, Commerce and Science, Mumbai.

Maithreyi Krishnaraj, Former Director, Research Centre for Women's Studies, S.N.D.T. Women's University, Mumbai.

Radhika Seshan, Faculty Member, Department of History, University of Pune, Pune.

C.R. Das, Assistant Professor in History, Competitive Examination Centre, University of Pune, Pune.

Umesh A. Kadam, Lecturer, Department of History, University of Pune, Pune.

Index